Travelers

. . . .

The Meaningful Journey

The Traveler

When have you arrived?

Your journey seems endless

When did you finally pronounce the word "home"

Without closing your eyes?

When have you arrived?

Tell me a secret

Have you ever left?

Travelers

· · · · · · ·

The Meaningful Journey

RÉGENT JEAN CABANA

TURNING
STONE
PRESS

First published in 2012 by
Turning Stone Press, an imprint of
Red Wheel/Weiser, LLC
With offices at:
665 Third Street, Suite 400
San Francisco, CA 94107
www.redwheelweiser.com

ISBN (paperback): 978-1-61852-028-9
ISBN (hardcover): 978-1-61852-027-2

Cover design by Jim Warner
Cover photographs:
Bicycle: Darko Sikman/Shutterstock.com
Palms: Photopixel: Shutterstock.com

Printed in the United States of America
IBT
10 9 8 7 6 5 4 3 2 1

Table of Contents

Chapter 1: The Calling   1
    To Find One's Rhythm   20
    To Travel Light   25
    To Allow Things to Happen   30
    To Understand the Other   34
    Advice to Would-Be Travelers   37

Chapter 2: The Journey   39
    Departures and Returns   43
    Imaginary and Real Journeys   50
    The Threshold: Where and When?   57
    Why Travel?   60
    Advice to Would-Be Travelers   71

Chapter 3: The Traveler   73
    History of Travel   75
    Travelers of 1997–1999   81
    The Bond of Travel   92
    What Is Home?   95
    Advice to Would-Be Travelers   97

Chapter 4: The Other   99
    Friendship and Tolerance   105
    The Concept of Culture   114
    Advice to Would-Be Travelers   122

Chapter 5: Transformations   123
   Mental Maps   128
   Terra Australis Incognita: Creativity and
     Authenticity   153
   To Be Human   156
   Legacy: The *Anima Mundi*   160
   Advice to Would-Be Travelers   163

Epilogue: The Life Well Lived   165
   Final Advice to Would-Be Travelers   169

This book is dedicated to the Traveler
inside each of us.

~ 1 ~

The Calling

It is well past midnight. The bright moon rays of the Southern Hemisphere illuminate the dirt road in front of me. I am walking hastily, half amused, half fearful, and naked. Was that a gunshot I heard in the distance? I glance in her direction. She, too, is naked, walking next to me, her motionless face showing no trace of concern. I wonder how she could be so beautiful at a moment like this. Suddenly she accelerates while grabbing my left arm.

"This way, this way, quick." We leave the road to cut into the middle of the sugarcane field. "My friend, she lives over there, she'll give us clothes to wear."

"Too bad," I say, "you look gorgeous." She smiles. I swear never to forget this night. We arrive at the doorstep. She knocks on the door. It opens. We are safe. I am relieved, momentarily. Was that another gunshot I heard in the distance? It would take me three more days to make it back to the hotel. When I did I was smiling and had clothes on.

I had met her two days before when I arrived at Nadi on the island of VitiLevu, the largest of the Fiji archipelago. As a single man traveling around the world, meeting local women was rarely a problem. What was problematic was the relationship: unrealistic expectations on both sides slowly dissolved the glue that binds a relationship. While the glue was fast acting, it was seldom long lasting. Unspecified promises also eroded the glue. What I considered a meager budget of $10 to $12 a day did not convince her I was not rich, particularly as it amounted to the weekly salary of some islanders. Neither was getting around using public transportation and walking instead of taking taxis. And she was right. To everybody else in the islands, I was an odd wealthy individual who traveled the world and does not need to work. Early in my travels I had given up explaining how I prepare for this experience and how broke I would be when I returned home.

"And why do you travel?" she once asked.

"To meet people like you," I answered.

I think I have forgotten her name. I remember it had the fascination of foreign sounds I could never pronounce correctly. It is almost as if she were a different person each time I uttered her name. How convenient never to have known her exact name. That night, that moon-filled night, we walked late in the countryside on the outskirts of town. The night was warm, clear and enticing. We arrived at a sugarcane field. There were no houses around. No one to be seen or heard. Soon we were lying down, side-by-side, naked. This is when I heard the hurried steps of what sounded like a very heavy man. I looked up and caught a glimpse of the shiny barrel of a shotgun pointing at the moon.

"He is after you," she said. "Don't get up, don't move."

"Do you know him?"

"Yes, yes, he wants to kill you. . . . Maybe kill me too."

I remained entirely motionless for what seemed a long time. Finally the sound of hurried steps became weaker.

"Hurry, hurry," I told her, "get your clothes and let's go." I looked around. "Where are our clothes?"

"Somewhere! Somewhere! He is a crazy man! He will kill you! No time, no time . . . Go, go!"

The clothes stayed in the cane field. We soon reached the road. The soles of my feet were burning. My heart was racing while my mind was busy assessing this unusual situation. My stopover in Fiji was the second leg of a trip around the world I had started some five months before. Now here I was, naked, walking in the middle of a sugarcane field to escape the anger of a big man (Fijians are "big men" physically as well as by title) with a shotgun in his hands while reflecting on my motivation to travel by myself to places I used to read about in *National Geographic* magazines as a child growing up in Sherbrooke in the French-speaking province of Québec.

Adventure was calling and its language was universal. Its appeal was not merely a shotgun heard in the distance over sugarcane near the town of Nadi in Fiji, or the sight of my attractive companion walking by my side. It was also the throb of my heart quickening my thought process while I walked rapidly toward my salvation, toward clothing. There is nothing like a little adventure to help one think clearly. The night was undeniably beautiful and exciting. I was stark naked and my mind was filled with questions and thoughts to consider. "Later, later," said a soft voice inside my head. "Keep walking, keep listening." But I could not help thinking that soon I would be alone again with plenty of time to reflect on the events of the night. Travelers always have plenty of time to reflect. I couldn't wait to start.

Time for reflection came soon enough. A few days after the Nadi episode, I went to a tiny Fijian island for three days and three nights. I didn't even know its name or where exactly it was located. There are 322 islands in the Fijian archipelago. I just boarded a boat one fine early morning and after a few hours of calm sailing I heard the captain say, "That's your destination; I'll pick you back up in three days. Be ready or the next boat may be a long time to come." It was probably on this very small tropical island in Fiji that I became a full-fledged Traveler. It was at this particular moment in my self-assigned mission to see and understand the world better that I began to weigh the motivations and consequences of my undertaking. Why do I travel like I do? What about other Travelers? Do they go through similar experiences? My time on the "six-minute island," which was the name I came up with after I realized I could walk around it in about six minutes, was probably the longest time, that is psychological time, I have ever spent anywhere in my life.

It was beautiful on this island. I spent most of my nights sleeping on the beach looking up at the wide starry sky. I had never seen anything like it before. By then, I thought I knew the Southern Hemisphere sky fairly well. I recalled the first time I laid eyes on the sky below the equator; I was in Argentina. I thought I had lost my groundings. No Northern Cross (star), no Big or Little Dipper; instead the Southern Cross, the constellation of Argo Navis, which is the ship sailed by Jason and the Argonauts, and the stars in Carina, representing the keel of the ship. At least, there was the familiar Milky Way, some 400 billion familiar stars.

But here on this island, too small to be on any map, the sky above my head was so spectacular that I thought I had crossed another threshold beyond which the familiar stars disappear among a multitude of new constellations.

The magnificence of my environment was overwhelming. Nonetheless, it was there, on this singular paradise on earth, that I hit rock bottom for three long days and three long nights. It was there that I experienced the dark night of my soul for three interminable days. I lay on the beach for hours on end, day and night, thinking that I could vanish and no one would ever notice. I did vanish for three days, but happily I noticed. I came back on time to catch the boat back to life.

"Hitting rock bottom" or "hitting a wall" were expressions used by Travelers I would interview four years later while doing research on Travelers for my Ph.D. dissertation. I use a capital "T" to refer to travelers who chose to travel by themselves around the world on a budget and for a long period of time. My research, conducted from 1997 through 1999, uncovered key experiences sought by Travelers and the values associated with these experiences. Ethnographic fieldwork provided a much-needed analytical distance from my own experiences as a Traveler as well as insights into the culture to which I also belong. Indeed, one of the key experiences Travelers go through during their time on the road is "hitting rock bottom." I did not know about it when I hit rock bottom on the six-minute island.

I will come back to this key concept experienced by all Travelers later on in the book. But for now, I would like to quote Paul, a Traveler from Germany. This is how he describes his experience of hitting rock bottom. He refers to it as "hitting a wall."

"On this day, I hit a wall, a thick and solid wall, and I could not climb it or walk around it. I had to take it apart brick-by-brick, and it was like each damn brick was one aspect of my life I did not want to look at before. It was painful. It took me a long time, and for a long time while traveling in Borneo I was so depressed. I felt that I was lost in the jungle of my mind, just like the jungles of the island. But now I know that it was necessary, and I feel better for having been through this nightmare. After that experience, I never traveled the same way again, never took anything or anyone for granted anymore. For me, hitting this wall was a turning point in my life. Now, I can appreciate my life, my travels, my friends and family, everything, everything I now appreciate better."

Neither did I know that upon my return to my life in the United States, I would be unhappy in my professional and personal life, finding issues with many of daily life acts I had never questioned before. I remember getting up in the morning, sometimes forgetting to have coffee, one of my favorite moments of any day, on the road or at home. I was going through "reverse cultural shock," which is often experienced by Travelers and anthropologists alike when they go back home—another phenomenon I discovered during my research on Travelers. This is probably what the French romantic writer René de Chateaubriand (1768–1848) refers to when he describes how upon his return home he soon found himself more isolated in his own country than he had ever been on foreign soil.[1]

The return home is a struggle for most Travelers. I was depressed. It was during my two years in Atlanta where I worked as a Cultural Attaché for the Québec Government that I resolved to find out more about the culture

---

1. Chateaubriand's René, in the short novel of the same name, voiced his feeling of isolation upon his return home to France after a sojourn among the Natchez of Louisiana. René was published in 1802.

of Travelers, a culture I knew a lot about as an insider, as a member of this culture, but very little from an analytical point of view. I wanted to step out of that culture in order to assess and understand it better. That's the reason I went back to graduate school in 1997.

I was thirty-three years old when I boarded a plane to Cairo, the first stop on my world journey. Perhaps I had made that decision in response to a midlife crisis I felt tightening up my throat every time I put on a tie to go to work in the morning. Was it not what Elliot Jacques (1917–2003), the Canadian psychoanalyst, had in mind when he coined the term "Midlife Crisis"?[2] It may have been my creative response to the unwavering life cycle during which we all need to make adjustments here and there in order to bring fresh meaning and enthusiasm to our endeavors. My age also put me in the second age group of Travelers (thirty to forty-nine years old), probably the fastest-growing of the three age groups I devised for the purpose of my study.

The first group, eighteen to twenty-nine, is the largest as well as the "traditional" backpacker/student Traveler. The third group, fifty to seventy-five, is also growing rapidly but its numbers were still relatively small in the late nineties. Over the course of my research I conversed with over 250 Travelers and over thirty other types of travelers and tourists (as a point of comparison). I conducted forty-seven in-depth interviews of sixty to ninety minutes each and over 100 informal interviews. I also led three focus groups during fieldwork in Mexico and New Orleans. These interviews, along with recorded

---

2. Elliot Jacques was an organizational psychologist. He came up with the concept of midlife crisis in 1965 to describe the midlife transition experienced by people who are no longer young and soon to enter old age.

participant observation activities, constituted the core data of my study.

I also interviewed less-experienced Travelers before or at the very beginning of their trip. I talked to more experienced Travelers in between trips or at various stages of their journey, as well as upon their return home at various periods after the completion of their travel, from immediately after their return to as long as four years after. Seasoned Travelers rarely spend more than two years before embarking on another journey. I have also talked to Travelers of all ages; the youngest was seventeen, the oldest seventy-five. The Travelers' nationalities also covered a wide spectrum of nations (France, Holland, Switzerland, England, Israel, Norway, Sweden, Japan, Italy, Australia, New Zealand, Canada, the United States, Germany, Spain, Croatia, Finland, Argentina, Brazil, Chile, Taiwan, Turkey, South Korea, India, Ireland, Mexico).

All of this investigative and analytical work would come years later and none of it was nearly as important as working through my personal issues when I hit a wall on the six-minute island. Gazing at the night stars, I began to sketch my life itinerary: What had happened before the six-minute island and what could happen after? For three days I disappeared and felt suspended in time, floating above the now, reviewing the track of life, of my life. My Pacific island became the center of the world and the center of the world was nowhere. I closed my eyes and dreamed of my life.

I grew up in the blue-collar neighboorhoods in the eastern part of Sherbrooke, a medium-size city in the eastern townships of the French-speaking province of Québec in Canada. Sherbrooke was largely an ethnically homogeneous city where the vast majority of residents spoke French while living on streets with names such as Johnson (the street I grew up on), Wellington, King, and Galt. A small but influential English-speaking minority lived on these streets, mostly in the northern part of the city. My father, an electrician, sometimes did work for a friendly Lebanese man who served very strong, very sweet coffee in very small cups. My father loved it. I do too now.

I wanted to be an archeologist, a spy (and/or diplomat) or a monk growing up, though not necessarily in that order. I discarded thoughts of a potential career as a professional hockey player or Catholic priest. The latter would have been a spirited choice for the youngest boy of a large Catholic family (did not all Catholic families need a priest to save their souls?) and the former a natural choice for a French-speaking Québécois who was taught how to ice skate by his mother when he was two years old. Above all, though, I dreamed of travels to foreign lands.

I kept a flashlight underneath my pillow. I read voraciously, mostly while the rest of the family slept. This is how I traveled when I was young. And, according to my mother, how I was going to ruin my eyesight. The words and ideas I found in books sparked my imagination. I had a strong desire to learn about other places and other peoples. One day, when I was about 12, my father came home with a collection of old *National Geographic* magazines. I wanted to visit those wonderful places I saw in lavish colors.

At eighteen, I took my first overseas trip to Spain. The official reason was to study Spanish for a month in Cuenca through a language program organized by the Lasalle College of Montréal. I studied for a week and then took off with a friend from home for the remaining three weeks. We accidentally got separated early in our journey while crossing the Strait of Gibraltar on our way to Ceuta and Morocco.

During his travels in Morocco my friend got beaten by a taxi driver and had his money stolen by a police officer. I met and fell in love with a pretty girl while relishing the warm exotic surroundings of a new, mysterious and somewhat incomprehensible world. I didn't see my travel companion again until we boarded the plane back to Montréal. But my adventures in Spain and Morocco already haunted me. I was hooked. It was upon returning home from this trip that I traced on a globe an itinerary around the world I would undertake one day.

I did not really learn English until I left home at nineteen to study in Victoria, British Columbia. I studied Psychology and completed a B.A. in Comparative Literature. I then moved to planet New Orleans where I taught French as a second language in the city's public schools for two years before I began my work as an educational supervisor for the French Program of the State Department of Education of Louisiana. I also got married in France (my wife was French) and went on my honeymoon with my father and brother (and my wife) in Switzerland and Italy.

Three years later I became a spy. Did I say spy? I meant diplomat, of course. Nevertheless, I did work for the Foreign Service of the Québec government for nine years in the United States, mostly in the capacity of public relations officer or cultural attaché. I also completed an M.A. in Urban Studies during that time and divorced my wife. My thesis looked at the lives of the Cajuns of Southeast Louisiana during the transition from rural to urban and suburban life and how their culture, including lifestyle, values, language, and religion, had been altered.

January 7, 1993 is a very special day in my life. It was the day I began a journey that took me around the world for eighteen months. I made all the travel arrangements by myself, sublet my apartment in New Orleans, and put my car in storage. I carefully selected a backpack that also converted into a suitcase. I was aware of the negative image backpackers have in some countries. I traveled alone. My father came twice to travel with me for about three weeks at a time. My eldest brother also joined my father and me in Singapore. Even though I had already traveled a good deal before 1993—in North America, Mexico, South America, and Western Europe—these trips never lasted more than four or five weeks. Some of them were taken alone, others with my ex-wife or with friends. But it was in 1993 that my life took a new direction when I interrupted a seven-year career with the Québec Foreign Service in order to travel the world. My job, upon my return home, was not guaranteed.

When I returned home, I resumed my career in the Foreign Service, working there for another two years before I resigned. Thereafter, I traveled for two months in Mexico, Belize, and Cuba, followed by four months in Asia, before embarking on a doctoral program in January 1997 at the University of New Orleans. As a graduate assistant, I have organized and conducted study tours for graduate students in Mexico and Canada. I still do today. I ask each of my students to keep a journal during the course of their ten-day study. I always read their journals, looking for clues that could reveal their state of mind while engaged in the activity of traveling and learning. "Traveling with a purpose" is an expression some of my students have used to describe the learning process that takes place during their studies in Mexico or Canada.

Writing this book about travel is a journey for me. It took me about two months to read the travel notes I had scribbled in some thirty small notebooks. Sometimes I could read my hasty writing only with difficulty; at other times the ink had faded or what I read barely made sense. Yet most of the time I could follow my thought process clearly. While in countries such as Israel, Egypt, India or Nepal I had written something every day and took copious notes on a variety of topics that interested me. I also kept a faithful record of my own ideas, impressions, and feelings. To my surprise, I also found when reviewing my notes that while visiting the beautiful Polynesian Islands or the Southern Islands of Thailand I had forgotten to write anything at all for days and even weeks. Maybe paradise is not conducive to note taking. Do we not say that happy people have no story to tell?

It was years later after I completed my trip around the world, that I began to understand why I made the decision in 1993 to travel extensively by myself and for a long period of time. Doesn't everyone want to travel around the world? Perhaps. What other Travelers have told me is exactly what I felt at the time I set out on my world journey: "I had to do it!" The desire to travel was much stronger than any other desire at the time and, therefore, I had no choice but to make it happen. I remember feeling that this trip, this journey, came at a pivotal time in my life and that because of it my life would be changed entirely. Learning takes many shapes and forms, and I have learned and still learn in so many different ways. However, at that particular time in my life, I felt that I would learn best by traveling. Like most Travelers, I wanted to learn about the world, about other people, and about myself.

I did not have specific questions I wanted answered. I had a specific itinerary but it changed many times, not so much in the destinations chosen as the time I had planned to spend in each place. With the passage of time, the structure of the trip simply collapsed, making room for improvisation. I did, however, have a general idea of what I wanted to accomplish, and it was a simple and straightforward plan: to go places I had never been and to meet people I had never met.

I believe that the answers you get depend upon the questions you ask. Formulating questions is a long and difficult task. It is much more difficult than finding answers. Good questions produce good answers, which in turn generate more questions. A final answer to any good question is, to me, the most depressing thought. Though I didn't have specific questions at the outset of my trip in 1993, I was aware of a few personal issues. Working on my dissertation made me more proficient at phrasing questions.

It also made me realize that I had lived with "my issues" all my life; during my travels these issues became crucial, probably because I had more time to think about them. On the road, I would begin to formulate my issues as ideas related to travel, my chosen avocation, as they became intuitively or metaphorically significant to me. This process was only the beginning. These ideas, my issues, also became an essential part of this book. Here they are articulated as questions:

1. What is more real, the world inside or the world outside? I remember as a teenager asking myself the following question: What is real, the world inside of me, the one I see when I close my eyes, or the world

outside, the world I see with my eyes open? What is reality, I thought? This self-interrogation and puzzlement that I formulated in a short poem some forty years ago has never left my awareness since. It has accompanied me during a life of traveling and has helped shaped many of my epiphanies as well as my hopelessness either on the road or sitting comfortably in the living room of my home. And it is the heart and soul of this book.

2. Who am I? The query into the complexities of this prototypical question is universal yet very personal. What is the sense of balance between the universal and the personal me? How or where to find it? Who am I as a Traveler? What motivates me? What activities am I engaged in on the road?

3. Who are other people? How is this Other different than me? How is the Other similar? What is the meaning of culture? Of authenticity? How is the encounter with the Other changing who I am? How is it changing the Other? Why am I traveling the world to meet the Other?

4. What is our collective memory? How do we form memories? What is the history—heritage—of the Traveler in the Western tradition?

5. What or where is home? What is home when on the road? Why is home such a key concept for the Traveler? Is home tied to time and space?

Readers probably understand by now that travel is my passion and that it was my lengthy journey in 1993 to 1994 that was largely responsible for my beginning and ongoing reflection on the richness of the Traveler's experiences, the literal and symbolic teaching travel dispenses, and the pivotal role it came to play in my life. This reflection on and awareness of the meaning of travel, and of my personal travels, really began on the six-minute island in Fiji; this book is the product of that reflection. When you travel by yourself, when you travel for a long period of time, and when you want to see the world on a budget, you bring in line certain experiences that are hardly available when you travel in other modes. This is not to say the other traveling experiences are less rich or less desirable. No, only different.

Traveling with my wife is also a great pleasure. Nonetheless, traveling by myself is, for me, a necessity that cannot be replaced by anything else. All the Travelers I have interviewed underscored the unique aspects of traveling by themselves and how it is an indispensable part of their lives.

I am addicted to travel. More precisely, I am addicted to journeying. And, like any true addiction, one can never be cured of it. You can only learn to live with it and try to keep it under control. You can also try to understand it better. Some people choose to center their lives around work, or family, or a place they truly love. Most of my life has revolved around the opportunity to travel, the appeal of the journey and the fascination with the other place and the other person. I am not the only one.

British novelist Lawrence Durrell (1912–1990) could not find the proper word to describe the condition of a person addicted to the appeal of the islands. He decided to invent it. The word is *islomania*.[3] An islomaniac is

---

3. British novelist, poet, and travel writer Lawrence Durrell moved to the Greek island of Corfu in 1935. It was during his stay on the island that he wrote the so-called Corfu Trilogy and coined the word *islomaniac*.

contented only when on an island or knowing that he will soon be going to an island. In other words, if he is not already there, an islomaniac would be willing to sacrifice anything to get to an island. The same is true for the Traveler and the appeal of the journey. Maybe the word *journeymania* can be ascribed to the condition of the Traveler. He is happy only when on a journey or when preparing for the journey.

Travelers like me are everywhere. The majority are willing to sacrifice a great deal to have only one more chance at this great game of the journey. The lure of the game is to come back home transformed. And you have to come back home because who will endorse this transformation if you never came back? The peril is to lose oneself in the process itself and to forget that the great journey is framed at one end by the departure and at the other end by the return. If someone does not complete the process, if one never returns home, literally or symbolically, the meaning of the journey dissipates into thin air. The story of a Traveler—my story—is about the journey, it is about departures and returns, about transformations and the lure of the road.

I have often thought of travel as a metaphor for our life journey. It is an important theme in my ongoing effort to better understand the Traveler, the Other, and myself. The reader of this book will find that it is composed of three elements: 1) a very personal intuitive reflection on travel and travel as a metaphor for life, 2) a description of the history and culture of Travelers, and 3) my story as a Traveler.

"This is my friend Sina," she casually said to me. "This is Rayan, he needs clothes." I guess my name too was vague to my naked friend. We walked in and sat down on a sofa as if we were coming to a dinner party. Her friend disappeared briefly. What am I to talk about? Make chitchat conversation?

"How are you doing?" I asked.

"Very well, thank you. And you?" Thank God Sina came back before I could answer. She was carrying clothes for both of us. I don't know why I asked to go into a private room to change. What silly behavior we are capable of under uncommon circumstances! I did not want to go back to my hotel room yet. What if the big man knew where I stayed?

"My sister is getting married, do you want to come?" asked Sina. "You will be safe there."

"When is it?"

"It started yesterday but will continue for more days."

"How many days?"

"I don't know, maybe four more."

I went and stayed three days. We ate periodically and drank kava kava continually. Kava kava is a mildly narcotic beverage made of the masticated roots of an herb that grows as a tall shrub in the Pacific islands. This shrub is a member of the pepper family and was named the "intoxicating pepper" by explorer James Cook (1728–1779). It contains soporific alkaloids and is a sedative, a diuretic, and a muscle relaxer. It plays an important role in the social and religious life of island inhabitants, especially during occasions that mark a new beginning or ending such as births, weddings, and funerals. My initiation to kava kava was a very pleasant experience. While the eldest daughter of the village chief prepared the drink and the other women assembled together in a large room in the house, I was invited to sit next to the chief, among the men.

We sat cross-legged on floor mats underneath a thatched roof that had been specially installed for the occasion. The kava kava was prepared in a large wooden bowl (*tanoa*) that was set in front of the chief. Before he helped himself from the bowl using a halved coconut shell (*bilo*), the chief clapped his hands vigorously once. He then drank the muddy water liquid in one long sip, lowered the bilo onto the floor and clapped three more times before handing it to me while talking at the same time.

"You, too, have to do like the chief," said my companion sitting to my left.

I obliged. It tasted like mud and I probably grimaced a little. If I didn't care that much for the taste, I soon loved its effects. First my lips, then my facial muscles, my limbs, even my fingers and toes felt slightly numbed and deliciously relaxed. Just what I needed after last night in the sugarcane field, I thought to myself. The chief was still talking, telling some kind of story I couldn't understand since he was speaking in Fijian.

"Your turn will come," said my new friend.

"Turn?! What turn?"

"Your turn to tell a story or sing a song."

I cannot sing, absolutely cannot, unless I'm all by myself. But I did tell a story when my turn came, late in the night or early in the morning. I told the sugarcane story, of the escape without clothes on, the beautiful silver moon rays bouncing off the barrel of a shotgun. I told them about the calling, about my burning desire to travel the world. Everybody laughed, or at least those who could understand English laughed at the story they probably thought I had just made up for the occasion. The others, the ones who couldn't understand English, laughed too, probably because kava kava tastes better when you laugh. We told each other stories all night long until we fell asleep on the floor mats just before breakfast was served. We did it again the following night, and the following. I went back to my hotel room after the third night, with clothes on, without hearing or seeing another shotgun. I quickly put all my belongings in my backpack and left the hotel.

I was in Hong Kong, about two months before I went to Fiji, when I called my girlfriend back in New Orleans. Our conversation lasted a little longer than usual and ended with my words "Don't worry, I'm coming back in a couple of days." I didn't really want to go back. By then I had traveled to Egypt, Israel, India, Nepal, the United Arab Emirates, China, and Hong Kong. I had found my rhythm and felt quite comfortable with myself on the road. When I had first started on my trip around the world, I was nervous: Can I really do this? Was it my calling? The first month in Egypt and Israel was difficult. I was looking for my rhythm. I think I found it in India sometime during the second or third month. Travel in India is never easy but it certainly provides great opportunities to find your rhythm.

But my girlfriend told me that she was sick, terribly sick. I interrupted my trip, flew home to spend one full week listening to her talking and talking and still talking more about her mysterious illness. Talking made her feel better, so much better that she didn't need me anymore. In fact, she didn't want a boyfriend anymore. She had found a girlfriend instead.

Once her mysterious illness was cured, I went to Québec to spend a couple of weeks with my family, a few days in New York to see a friend, and then I was off to

Tahiti, the Cook Islands and Fiji, the first three stopovers on the second leg of my journey. No wonder my rhythm was somewhat off as I arrived at Papeete airport in Tahiti and a bit later at Nadi airport in Fiji. Because, you see, we Travelers have tasks to carry out during our travels. It is the nature of the calling, which comes with responsibilities. The first one is to find our rhythm. I looked for my rhythm in the sugarcane field; I looked for it in the kava kava and in the unintelligible stories told during three long and delicious nights. I looked for it anywhere, everywhere. For a Traveler, just as for an athlete, finding one's rhythm is crucial. My search took me to the six-minute island where I finally found it the minute I left the island. Where had it been all this time?

Task #1: To Find One's Rhythm

I love golf. When I warm up at the golf range before a round, I first take several slow and somewhat nonchalant swings. My concentration is on the movement of the body, the flow of the motion, and the easiness of the process of hitting a small white ball. I do not pay attention to how to do it or where to hit the ball. My full attention is focused on the process itself, on finding the comfort zone where mind and body are completely at ease, working in unison, entirely focused on the task at hand. The task at hand is finding one's rhythm.

The golfer has found his rhythm when the trained motion of the body flows naturally and the mind shows no sign of strain. The rhythm is found in relaxation. Only when he has found his rhythm can the golfer confidently move on to perfecting different strokes. There are naturally countless degrees of excellence, but when the golfer's rhythm appears impeccable, his technical dexterity faultless, his mental sharpness immaculate, we use expressions such as being "in the zone" or "in the flow" to describe the inimitable style of the athlete, the transcendence of his performance and his extraordinarily sound state of being.

Mihaly Csikszentmihalyi (1934–)[4] developed the psychology of the optimal experience around the notion of flow, when one's concentration is on the process itself and not on the goal. Abraham H. Maslow (1908–1970)[5] writes about the peak experience and Joseph Campbell (1904–1987) talks about the sublime or bliss in reference to the experience of the flow.[6] In the early stage of their journey, Travelers of all kinds are also trying to find their rhythm. They look for it in the novel places they visit. They try to decipher its contours from the facial lines of newly encountered peoples. They expect its appearance around the next corner, at the end of the next bus ride, waiting to be legitimately recognized and claimed as one's own. They look for it while contemplating the mystic attributes of the ageless Buddha sculpted in marble, gold, or jade, sitting alone, covered with dust, almost neglected in the corner of a small little-known temple or museum. Alas, if the inexperienced Traveler is seeking to find his rhythm in the outside world he is exploring, hoping for it to come to him from somewhere at some precise time as some kind of epiphany, the delusion of such a high expectation will sorely test his stamina. The

---

4. Mihaly Csikszentmihalyi. *Flow: The Psychology of Optimal Experience* (New York: Harper and Row, 1990).

5. Abraham Maslow. *Religions, Values, and Peak Experiences* (New York: Penguin Books, 1964).

6. American mythologist Joseph Campbell often used the phrase "follow your bliss" to encourage individuals to follow their own path and to be in touch with the life within each of us.

process then becomes a gritty experience. Such was the case for Renaud.

Renaud left France two weeks before I first met him in Guanajuato, Mexico. He was in his mid to late twenties. Trained as a photographer, he couldn't find stable work in France. He was quite resentful toward France's intricate administrative system that made it so difficult for a young man to start a career in photography. He was a good example of a dropoff: one who is waiting for a logical excuse to realize a dream he has been contemplating for a long time. Renaud's excuse was a lack of good work opportunities in France. His dream was to be a Traveler. For Renaud, as well as for many other Travelers I have spoken to since, being a Traveler is to step out of oneself and seek personal transformation in new environments and through new experiences. To be a tourist, said Renaud, is merely to be entertained by new environments and experiences.

Renaud did not want to be a tourist. Nevertheless, he was wearing a watch that he constantly looked at. He talked briskly, walked hurriedly and generally felt nervous about his situation. He was at the beginning of his journey and, in his words, was having a hell of a time adjusting to his newfound freedom on the road. He said, "Je dois trouver mon rythme" ("I have to find my rhythm"). For Renaud, finding his rhythm (or not being a tourist) meant disconnecting from France and walking like the locals, leisurely and unhurriedly. It was also, for him, to speak Spanish more fluently, to stop wearing a watch, and to be more tanned. "I just can't find my rhythm," he told me in French. "I can't seem to relax and be the Traveler I want to be. I feel like a damned tourist!" Renaud was the first Traveler I heard using the word "rhythm" in relation to travel. It was at the beginning of my fieldwork in

Mexico that I met him. I did not yet know how important this concept would turn out to be in my research. I hope Renaud did find his rhythm.

The Traveler's rhythm is to be found within oneself. Travelers, like athletes, always find their rhythm by experimenting with the feel of motion. How does it feel to move around, to go from this place to another place, to talk to these people today and others tomorrow? How is this outer motion a translation of inner motion (or vice versa)? How is physical mobility a reflection of psychological mobility (or vice versa)? Finding one's rhythm in the early stage of the journey is a blessing. But to find it at any stage of the journey is crucial. Not to find it is to sever the deep, rich, and evocative link between the worlds a man carries inside whenever and wherever he goes and the worlds encountered out there whenever and wherever he is.

By looking inwardly while moving outwardly, by slowing down one's own thought process while assimilating the multitudinous array of new sensual stimuli, by paying close attention to subjective feelings and hunches while traveling the objective world, a Traveler gradually comes to sense his rhythm and to claim it as his own. Once he does so, he is ready to embark on a very personal journey that will deepen and broaden his sense of who he is, what the world is, and what the intimate connection between the two means to him subjectively and to the world objectively. It is a never-ending education, but each individual journey taken brings him closer to a symbiotic understanding of who he is in the world and what the world is inside of him.

Is there really a difference between the Traveler and the world in which he is traveling? This is a genuine question and, like all good questions, one that can be answered from an endless array of perspectives. Each new angle provides a shade of meaning that is absent from all the others. There are no boundaries to the depth and width of the answers. Each of the answers uncovered is forever tattooed on the Traveler's body. For the Traveler, his body is a detailed map of the world he travels, with the oceans, rivers, mountains and valleys giving shape to his shoulders, belly, and groin. The voices he hears and the faces he sees run rambunctiously in his own blood. The Traveler truly has every right to claim the world as his home. His body and the world are the same.

For the Traveler, finding one's rhythm or not is the difference between a trip and a journey. For the Traveler, finding one's rhythm, trusting it and expanding its reach through the entire mind and body and onto the objective world he explores is to have a taste of transcendence with his feet firmly set on the ground. We can say that while on a journey, a Traveler is in a state of grace. That he truly travels inside the outside world.

I was very quiet on the boat back to Nadi. Even the captain noticed. He came to talk to me.

"What did they do to you on the island?" he asked.

"Nothing, Captain," I answered. "Nothing. I spent all my time looking at the stars; I didn't know you could count so many."

"Oh! The stars. I see, you like the stars."

"Yes, that's it," I said, "I like the stars."

The captain left. How was I going to tell him I had hit rock bottom (I didn't even know this expression then) or that I had been looking for my rhythm and had finally found it right here and now on his boat! I was drained but secretly happy. I had my rhythm and I could go on with my journey, indefinitely. Once again, I could see the light, perhaps the same light the captain saw at night in the starry sky.

Task #2: To Travel Light

I was back in Nadi. Why was I feeling naked? I felt more naked fully dressed than I had a few days earlier in the cane field without any clothes on. Strange. It was at this time that I decided to continue on traveling naked (figuratively speaking). "Light, light, travel light," I kept repeating silently to myself; this was my new mantra in the day and for weeks to come. "Empty your mind; let it be space, soaring space in and around you," I told myself softly over and over. I went to a local bar that evening. The band and the dancing were outstanding. After a few Fiji Gold beers, the words of a popular New Orleans brass band song came to mind: "My feet can't fail me now."

In New Orleans, dancing is as natural as breathing and you do a lot of it with your feet. However, in Fiji, it would be more accurate to say "my knees can't fail me now." Fijians, unlike the people of New Orleans, dance a lot with their knees, shaking and crossing them relentlessly. I tried to emulate them. My main shaking partner was a professional dancer and Miss Fiji some years back. She was a fantastic dancer and a beautiful woman. I thought it was odd that nobody else, all locals, asked her for a dance. Was it because everybody else was staring at my figurative nakedness? Are not all foreigners naked to the locals?

It is a liberating feeling to dance naked in front of strangers. The alcohol helping, I felt invincible, untouchable, until a stranger, a friend really, asked me if I knew who the woman I was dancing with was.

"Yes, yes, I know," I said, "she's a great dancer and a former Miss Fiji."

"That's right," he said, "and she's also the wife of the most jealous man in Nadi."

"What does he look like?" I asked, wondering if perhaps by some incredible coincidence he could be the same big man from the sugarcanes. "Is he a big man?"

"See for yourself," he pointed to a huge man entering the bar. "Here he is. He is the reason why none of us dance with that beautiful woman."

No, I didn't think he was the same big man, even though I had not really seen the man searching for us among the sugarcane stalks. This man must be even bigger, probably more dangerous. Carefully avoiding crossing his path, I quietly exited through the back door. I had learned my lesson well. Besides, I had seen fierce fights in Nadi's bars since my arrival and knew I wouldn't measure up. I fled the scene at the speed of light. I felt lightheaded. I looked back only when the motor of my scooter stopped running. It wasn't my mind that was light or empty, it was the gas tank.

At the beginning of my journey, the challenge of traveling alone with only a backpack all over the world was exhilarating. But soon I came to realize that I had too much baggage physically, intellectually, and emotionally. This recognition really hit home in Fiji. I started shedding some of my physical luggage. I ended up with a very small backpack. I felt lighter and more relaxed, in touch with my identity as a Traveler. I was amazed by how little I needed. It was a liberating feeling. Then I gave away my very heavy guidebooks. I began to relax. I stopped making travel plans or wanting to fulfill my tourist obligations.

The earlier challenge of traveling was slowly transforming itself into the joy of traveling. At last I knew what brought me joy while traveling. I had finally found the courage to trust my instincts, to stay in one small town just because I liked it and not worry about what else the guidebooks said I was missing. One evening after I had come back to my hotel after a light dinner, I looked at my open backpack resting on the small bed of my spartan hotel room in Nadi. What do I have inside, I wondered? Not much. A pair of slacks, shorts, socks, a couple of short-sleeve shirts, one long-sleeve, a light jacket, cap, a bathing suit, a small first-aid pouch, a Swiss knife, a small extensible lock, a travel-size alarm clock, a small toiletry bag, a shortwave radio, a small camera with no film, two pens and a notebook. Why is it so empty now when it had seemed almost impossible to close the day I left for my trip around the world? That day now seemed so long ago. What had happened between then and now?

The Traveler who has found his rhythm then has another all-important preoccupation. To travel swiftly, alertly, and purposefully, the Traveler must travel light. I love the fact that in the English language the word light means both "having little weight" or "something that makes vision possible." The meaningful journey requires both. How can one develop his vision if too much baggage weighs him down? Literally speaking, weight encumbers movement. Figuratively, it hampers the proper functioning of sight. How can one see well if his mind is not clear, free of unnecessary burdens? The essence of travel is to move. To move effectively, one needs to be as light as possible. The quest of the Traveler is to see the world. To see well one has to fill his mind with light, to "light up his mind." With clear vision and swift movement the

Traveler ceases to differentiate the body of the world from his own body.

In order to travel light, both literally and figuratively, the Traveler goes to great pains. This continuous transformative process that concerns the social and personal being of the Traveler begins rather simply with his physical possessions that he carries along in one or two backpacks or suitcases. One backpack on the back of the Traveler, like an extension of his body—or better, a detachable section of his being—is to me the quintessential image of the Traveler.

The question, then, is the following: How can I make myself lighter or what can I eliminate without feeling incomplete? Therefore, little by little, the backpack becomes lighter. In the process, thoughts and feelings associated with the physical objects discarded come under scrutiny. At the same time the mind, much too heavy at the beginning of the journey, sheds some of its weight. For the Traveler, the meaning of traveling light reaches dimensions never suspected prior to the departure, when the highest importance was placed on what one may need for the trip rather than what one must not burden himself with in order to move swiftly and see clearly.

If finding one's rhythm is tuning in to the exact frequency the depth of one's being emits and allowing it to radiate throughout the mind and body, traveling—feeling—light is to carry a diapason of this very private note to all activities, physical, intellectual, or emotional. Each Traveler moves to his own unique internal rhythm. Each backpack is always uniquely one's own. However, the scaling-down process is awaiting the Traveler who wants to journey further. Unless one travels naked, there is always something else to shed.

Hilda is from Norway. She is thirty-three years old. During a long and intimate interview in a small café on Magazine Street in New Orleans, Hilda explained to me that traveling solo was something she discovered accidentally. "I had no idea I could do it, never thought about it, really." One day, just days after she had left Norway, her traveling companion and best friend had to go back home unexpectedly. "I had only two choices," she told me, "either I went back with her or I made it on my own. I'm glad I chose to go on by myself."

That was three years ago. Since then, Hilda has been hooked on solo travel. "I enjoy traveling so much more now that I do it alone. It's more exciting and more unpredictable. There is very little I need, really. Only a small backpack, not much else. I don't think too much, I just go where I want and when I want. I have never experienced anything like this before. I feel free to be myself and to learn so much. I am so happy my friend had to go home and that I found myself alone. It was a little hard at first, you know, a woman by myself. But I'm not afraid anymore. Now, I always plan my trip alone. But I'm never alone. I meet so many interesting people."

Peter, twenty-six years old and from Germany, had the following thoughts about traveling solo: "Traveling by myself is so much easier and so much more interesting. I can think my own thoughts; see inside of me what matters. You see, traveling like I do, there is no place to hide from myself. I had to learn to like myself better . . . you know, if I did not like myself, I would send myself home in a hurry. And that would be the end of it. But no, now

I respect who I am better because of my travels. And I feel good because I know I need little in life. I understand now what matters. It's not what you have but who you are and how you relate to other people. That's all. It's all here (pointing to his head) and here (pointing to his heart). Now, I know."

On the road or at home, one's consciousness is always in movement. To catch oneself in the motion of consciousness, to alter one's inner or outer conditions, to move through outer space and outer time as easily as we move through inner space and inner time is to recognize the journey. To be present in the moment when inner and outer movements occur in synchronization is to experience the luxurious sensuality of the journey. There is no pleasure that I know greater than the enjoyment of traveling light. It can happen anywhere and at any time. One needs only to be aware of the light.

Task #3: To Allow Things To Happen

The walk alongside my scooter was not the most enjoyable night walk of my time in Fiji. Nevertheless, after a few minutes of this unwanted bedtime exercise, I started smiling and soon I was laughing out loud at the silliness of my behavior. It had suddenly dawned on me that all I seemed to have accomplished since my arrival on the island was to pursue beautiful women and be pursued by their jealous boyfriends. What's going on here? I finally reached my hotel just before dawn. I went straight to bed and woke up hungry and with a massive hangover. I was resolved to do something good. I invited two Fijian friends I had met a week ago for lunch. They were cousins.

"May I bring my aunt along?" asked Nyla.

"Of course you may."

I let my friends choose the restaurant. They decided on a small popular eatery located on the main street downtown where they served excellent and inexpensive local food. I was quite pleased with my friends' choice since I was traveling on a very limited budget. There, I told myself, we can have great food that I can afford. It was an open-air restaurant and the view from our table allowed us to people-watch while eating. Even better, I thought, as I love to observe passersby.

While Nyla was perusing the menu, it happened that another cousin passed by. I invited the cousin to join us. Then, two nephews also passed by. We had to get more chairs. A grandma and someone else soon showed up. Shortly afterward, another relative of some kind joined us. In Fiji, you cannot turn down family members who wish to share your food. I had to ask for another table. I excused myself for a few minutes to run to the nearest ATM machine. I probably spent my entire weekly budget for that lunch. We had a great time; one happy hungry family. I felt good about myself, about everything really, including the silliness of the past week. At last, I have come to accept my identity. I am a Traveler. At last, I have learned to allow things to happen and not to worry about why they happen.

The notion of the controlled accident in Chinese philosophy is the idea of allowing things to happen by themselves while always keeping a watchful eye on the course of their manifestation. The Traveler who has found his rhythm and who is engaged in the process of traveling light sooner or later becomes interested in the notion of the controlled accident. The English word *serendipity* is the closest approximation to it but doesn't include the concept of looking indirectly at signs of things to come.

The Traveler, while traveling, is engaged in an activity that transcends his usual sense of self. His personal identity spills out into the world he is visiting, contributing to the formation of events he experiences as objective happenings, but which inexplicably bear his own signature. "Things happen." But the things that happen also are. Although unrecognized, they were first in a state of being as potential events but certainly familiar to the Traveler's own state of being. The art of the controlled accident is the art of recognition. It is to know beyond doubt that what happens out there has always been present inside, deep inside the Traveler's psyche.

So many Travelers I talked with had stories about how their adventures on the road brought answers to personal issues or conflicts they thought they had forgotten. They were not looking for these answers, at least not consciously or actively, but prolonged solo travel will put the Traveler in situations that have him confront these personal issues or conflicts. It is only a matter of time before the Traveler recognizes what is happening. Seasoned Travelers are always paying attention to what is going on around them. They know they are not strangers to their environment.

Peter from Australia was in his mid-forties and had been traveling for more than a year when I met him in Mexico City. He knew about the "controlled accident." "The way I plan my trips," he said, "is by understanding that I am not in charge, really. Yes, I make plans, decide on where to go and how to get there, but the real kick is to know that someone else is overseeing your trip, and that someone else is you, the real you, I mean at the deepest level. You understand? And that deep you knows exactly what you want to do, what challenges you are ready to face. So, I have learned over the years, when I travel, to be ready, ready for whatever I have planned at the deepest level. Then, I just have to let it happen. But, consciously, I know nothing of it. I am in for the ride. But I have to be on the lookout, not to miss the opportunities."

Subsequently, Peter found himself one evening in a dark bar in a small town in Colombia. A man approached him and quietly asked for his money. He answered that he had no money. But the man insisted. This is when Peter noticed that the man was armed. He told him that he had about $10, just enough to buy him a couple of beers. "The man looked at me," Peter recalled, "he hesitated for a moment, looked at me again, closely, probably realized that I was telling the truth, and sat down on the stool on my right. We drank together, shared a couple of laughs, and then I left. You have to understand, I've always been afraid of being robbed or killed during a robbery. I don't know where this fear comes from, and I could have been robbed and killed that evening. But now, somehow, I'm not afraid of it anymore. My fear is completely gone."

Nancy from the United States, another Traveler I interviewed, spoke movingly about the mystical nature of traveling. She was in her mid-thirties when we met. She talked about how she feels one with the universe when she travels, even during her darkest moments on the road. One such moment came a little over two months after she had left for a six-month trip to Southeast Asia, shortly after her father had committed suicide. It was when she hit rock bottom. "One day," she explained, "it all became very clear. Why I had embarked on this trip; what I was running away from. I had to confront my fears, my anger, frustration, all those strong emotions toward my father. It was all there in front of me, crystal clear, no escape. That's why I left, traveled by myself. When it hit me, I realized that this was the experience I was seeking, this huge depression, in order to be made whole again. It felt like the whole universe had planned this for me. Or that I had planned it with the universe. I needed this. I had to let my feelings out, confront them and let them go. And I needed to do it by myself, alone. I did. I felt much better afterward, much better."

Task #4: To Understand the Other

"Hey, big man!" someone shouted. "Big man, yes, you, the big man."

I turned around, looking for the big man.

"No, no, you; I'm talking to you. You're the big man."

"Me?" I said, "I don't know you. Why are you calling me big man?"

"I am Nyla's cousin," he said. No, not another one, I sighed as he continued. "She told me about the big party at the restaurant yesterday; you're the big man, you invited my family, but why not me? That's what big men do: they treat people well, like you did yesterday. Nyla called you big man; I call you big man."

I had never been called a big man before. But I was starting to feel like a big man. And I wanted to act like a big man. I asked for his name and invited him for coffee and pastries.

"I'd like to get to know you better," I told Rumi. "Perhaps you're a big man, too."

He declined the invitation. The only explanation I came up with is that he was afraid I would expect him to pick up the bill. That is what big men do. But that was not what I meant, or was it? He probably misunderstood me.

While traveling, the Traveler's sense of who he is, both as an individual and as a member of a community, is constantly being defined and redefined by his encounters with the Other. The Other becomes the point of reference by which the Traveler defines who he is. Making his home in movement itself, his perception of the Other is often blurred or lacking in perspective. But he always strives to understand the Other because he intuitively senses that whatever he may comprehend about the Other is one more small piece that fits into the jigsaw puzzle of who he is and what the world is to him. If the whole world is contained in one grain of sand, as poet William Blake (1757–1827) says, certainly it is also contained in this single idea of who I think I am. Hindu philosophy offers the word *lila*, god playing hide-and-seek with itself and relishing in self-discovery after self-discovery.

The Traveler feels free. The Traveler feels joy. Tremendous joy and exhilarating freedom. The Traveler may always feel joy, because whatever is wrong, there is always one reason to rejoice, even though this only reason may be one's capacity to recognize the uniqueness of his sorrows. He also feels rootless and insecure. His social identity is in a state of flux. His personal identity is for trying on, as one may try on different clothes. His sense of belonging is tied to a community of passage where the only social indicator that really matters is one's capacity to empathize with fellow Travelers on their journey.

Travelers' social chat revolves around the Other: Other places, other peoples, and other times.

Travelers instinctively know that to understand the Other better is to understand oneself better. Each encounter with the Other sheds a little more light on one's identity. However, the Traveler often tends to forget that he too is an Other to everyone else. To be still in the midst of movement is to make no distinction between the Self and the Other. Travelers are compelled to move on unknowingly seeking the eye of the hurricane. The mystery of the Other is the mystery of self.

Alexander was a twenty-four-year-old Traveler from Canada. Even at this young age, he had traveled solo extensively in Central and South America, Africa, and Asia. He had made many friends in many different countries. What he told me about understanding the Other, about friendship across cultures, gave me reason to pause. Alexander said that his "travel friends" were very special to him because they taught him how to relax.

"What do you mean by that?" I asked.

"Before I traveled, I thought that I chose my friends or that they chose me. Now I realize that my friends are not so different than me and that if we both relax, just be who we are and take time to talk to each other, we'll probably end up understanding each other and being friends. It's that simple. Just relax."

Finding one's rhythm. Traveling light. Letting things happen. Understanding the Other. These are the tasks of the Traveler from the moment he leaves home to the moment he returns. If the calling is the lure of travel, meeting these tasks is its drive. The trip becomes a journey whenever the Traveler commits himself to addressing these tasks. Feeling free, happy, rootless and insecure are the conditions that affect the Traveler during the journey. The reward is to realize that one has never left home and that home is everywhere and any time one senses his own rhythm throbbing in the world out there.

Advice to Would-Be Travelers

Travel light. But do not forget to bring (social) adapters and (cultural) converters.

⤳ 2 ⤳

The Journey

They called me "big man," but I was unsure whether I wanted to be a big man or not. Were they expecting more parties, more generosity on my part? But I could not afford it. Will they understand my predicament? Or will I make false promises in order to maintain my big man status? For how long could I do this? Perhaps it was time to leave Fiji. After all, I am a Traveler; I have responsibilities and tasks to meet and promises to myself to keep. Is it not my nature to move on, to leave behind my newfound friends and unfulfilled hazy promises? Is this not the nature of the journey? These conflicting thoughts left me uneasy. I resolved to talk to Nyla and ask her advice on this delicate topic. I went to the hotel where she works.

"Nyla," I said, "I have to talk to you."

"I finish my work soon. Come back in one hour, we'll talk."

One hour, one hour, I repeated to myself, one hour did not mean much on the island. I should come back in two hours, perhaps three. I stepped out onto the street and unhurriedly made my way to my favorite coffee shop, vaguely preoccupied with the decision about when to go back to see Nyla. Caffeine seldom fails to quicken my thought process. I automatically grabbed my pen and notebook, ready for fresh insights. I ordered coffee and started writing immediately.

One word and then another, in French, then a string of unusual words, in English; where was this leading me? Perhaps another unpredictable poem? It had been quite a while since I had written my last short poem. It was at the Moon Walk in New Orleans. I was looking at the large ships passing by and thinking they had traveled on many oceans and anchored at many ports in many countries all over the world. I likened my thoughts to the passing ships, influenced by so many transient spaces and times, resting nowhere really, always longing for the next destination, somewhere else. But what are ships without rivers and oceans, the poem asked. They are lifeless thoughts. "My thoughts are the passing ships, but my heart is the ocean," concludes the poem.

The coffee came. I took a couple of sips and looked at the unexpected words I had set down on the white page of my notebook. Words such as adventure, misadventure, wonder, companionship, and autonomy were keywords to my state of mind at this particular moment in my journey. If there were no doubts in my mind that I was on a journey, the exact nature of the journey was not easy to fathom. I was obviously struggling with the ambivalent desire for companionship, commitment, dependability, and the seemingly opposed desire for a lack of restrictions— my alleged freedom and independence.

I was in a bind with absolutely no idea of how to resolve the conflict. I took one long last sip of coffee and waited for the caffeine to work its magic. Instead, my mind went blank, a blissful emptiness. It felt good. Time slipped out of my consciousness. Did I fall asleep drinking coffee? What had happened to the acute sense of awareness I usually experience with caffeine?

I made it back to the hotel where Nyla worked. "Nyla has gone home already," I was told.

Since I didn't know where Nyla lived, I had no choice but to come back the next day. I stepped out onto the street once more, a strong sense of déjà-vu filling my senses. Before I knew it I was again walking in the direction of the coffee shop. Not this time, I told myself. I stopped immediately, crossed the street and took the next street to the left. I had no idea where I was going. After walking for some time I felt hungry and stopped at a small grocery. I walked in, picked up some fruits and a drink and went to the cash register. There was Nyla standing in line.

"Nyla, what are you doing here?" I asked, very surprised to see her in the store.

"I live down the street," she replied, "I'm picking up groceries for tonight." She didn't seem surprised at all to see me in her neighborhood.

"Nyla, can I talk to you now? I'd like to ask you something."

"No problem, if you buy me ice cream, we can talk while we eat."

"Yes, of course, I'll buy you ice cream," I replied, thinking that I might end up buying ice cream for the whole neighborhood. I quickly checked my pocket to see how much money I had and concluded that it should be enough for at least twelve people. I ordered one chocolate and one vanilla. I knew very little about Nyla and had never asked questions about her family.

"You live in this neighborhood, with your family?"

"Yes, with my two daughters and husband." She hesitated slightly. "I have not seen my husband in three years; he lives in California. He works there as a gardener. I think he has a new wife in California. He's a good man; he sends us money every month."

"And you, Nyla, will you remarry?"

"What for?"

"Listen, Nyla, you called me a big man the other day. What does it mean?"

She did not falter in answering. "It means that I respect you."

"Is your husband a big man, too?"

"Yes," she said, "he sends us money."

"Who else is a big man?"

"My brother is. He takes care of our mother."

"Will I still be a big man if I have no money to buy you ice cream?" I persisted with a twinkle in my eye, determined to get to the bottom of this big man business.

"If you have no money, no problem; it's the size of your heart that counts, not the size of your wallet."

Nyla was a very kind and wise person; certainly she was a "big man," the most beautiful big man on the island. I had no more questions to ask her. I smiled broadly, looked straight into her eyes and announced that I was leaving Fiji in a few days.

"We'll have a farewell party," she said casually.

"Yes, that would be great," I responded slowly while mentally trying to calculate the financial damage my farewell party might bring. Perhaps I can leave before the party, I thought. After all, I travel on a budget. My journey was unfolding, almost without my noticing its presence.

Departures and Returns

One of the oldest journey stories we have on record is that of Gilgamesh, king of the ancient city of Uruk. The Epic of Gilgamesh, at least some of it, is believed to have been transcribed around 2000 BC. The cuneiform tablets bearing the story were found in the 1840s in the capital of the Assyrian Empire, the ancient city of Nineveh. I have never been there, yet. The legend tells the story of Gilgamesh who left his native land to travel to the edge of the world. Gilgamesh amassed all the learning about the world and about himself during his long journey, which bore its fruits only upon his return home and after he had written up his travel stories on twelve large flat clay tablets, Before his return, and before the symbolic transmission of Gilgamesh's knowledge for all to witness, the teaching of the journey (at times extracted at great risk) was useless. Without a return there is no journey.

But what is a journey? The English word *journey* comes from the French word *journée*, which means "a day." The word *travel* comes from the French word *travail* which means "labor." Travel is arduous. The rewards of travel do not come without effort. The dictionary defines the word *journey* as "travel or passage from one place to another." The word *passage* is, in my opinion, the one that best characterizes a journey. If we take a simple analogy, that of an iceberg, the tip of the iceberg represents the trip while the whole iceberg is the journey. Submerged and invisible to the naked eye is the passage, the place and time where and when the Traveler is transformed. What transforms a trip into a journey is the willingness of the Traveler to be aware of the presence of the passage and to allow its unimpeded course to shape his every physical and psychological movement. In other words, the Traveler is on a journey the moment he becomes aware of the passage.

The stages of the physical journey with its preparation, departure, the act of travel itself and the return home contain deep metaphorical links to the rhythms of man's life. Life (birth-life-death) as a journey is a powerful and evocative metaphor. One of travel's best-known aphorisms, that the essence of travel is to be found in the journey, alludes to the paramount importance of the process itself. Just as in life, with birth and death framing the "life journey" like two exclamation points, the travel journey is framed by the departure and the return. A myriad of life conditions combine in singular ways to form one's unique life. How one reacts to what seems to be given and creates something unprecedented out of those conditions is the story that interests us all: it is one's life story. Similarly, it is of small importance what countries we visit or how long we travel; what really matters is how we travel and what we make of the travels.

A journey starts with a singular movement. It is the departure from the ordinary, however one defines the ordinary. Death certainly represents the beginning of a journey, and so does birth. Stepping on a plane, bus, or boat can also mark the initiation of a journey. Most often, crossing some kind of threshold sets us on our journey: An ocean, the equator, or a state line. These crossings trigger a kind of inner mechanism that alerts our whole being to pay closer attention to what is happening. I suspect that the addiction to travel, which afflicts me and countless others, is ingrained somewhere in this inner mechanism that brings increased awareness to our senses and a renewed sense of purpose to our very existence.

A departure, even when most secretive, is invariably loaded with symbolism. Don Quixote left in the early dawn, telling not a soul of his errant peregrination and riding far away. Sancho Panza never said goodbye to his wife or children. The journey was to be a confidential agreement between the imaginative power (represented by Don Quixote) and the normal, ordinary strength (represented by Sancho Panza). No one else was to be alerted. If anyone else had known, the whole village would have laughed at Don Quixote and Sancho Panza. Nobody respected the knight anymore. And, above all, Don Quixote wished to become a celebrated knight.

Unlike Don Quixote, many of my own departures took place at airports where I was surrounded by thousands of other travelers, some like me initiating their own journey; others completing it. Still others, contented to take a trip, were casually sitting on top of their own iceberg looking out in the direction of the well-beaten path. On those occasions, I felt an instant bond with the crowd itself, with the collective "on the move" entity each of us nourished. I also felt lonely. I didn't know anyone there.

However, I felt profoundly privileged to be a part of this ceremonial event during which thousands of fellow travelers go through the motion of the departure or the return with all to witness one and one to witness all. And to think that in a couple of hours most of us would be gone to be replaced by others repeating the same ritual added to my sense of awe and sympathy. Where has everyone gone? What brave adventures awaited the old man who was sitting behind me, his seat now empty? Maybe this is what happens when we die and when we are born: we disappear somewhere and appear somewhere else. Perhaps we go to the closest airport when we are ready to die.

There is one particular departure that I remember well. It involved my family when I was eighteen years old. I remember it because I have a photograph of it. I'm standing in the middle of the photograph, wearing loose white pants tied with a brown and black stretch belt and a white shirt. I'm carrying a small light-blue denim bag slung over my shoulder. In my right hand are the plane tickets; in my left hand a notebook. A wristwatch my parents had given me is on my left wrist, but the time isn't visible. If memory serves it was a mid-morning flight from Dorval airport in Montréal to Vancouver. My parents are not in the picture, but they were there. Perhaps my father or mother took the picture. My godchild Alexandre is behind me and we can see the right arm and part of the right leg of my sister Suzanne. I'm wearing a broad smile. The mood of the whole scene is happy. My body is leaning slightly forward as if telling an observer—or the photographer—that I can vanish at any moment.

Not much has changed since that day in Dorval thirty-five years ago. I still can sense my body tingling all over while I wait for my plane at any airport in the world, with or without family or friends. I can almost feel it bending ever so slightly forward in anticipation of the departure, of going somewhere else. And I still carry a shoulder-strap bag in which I keep plane tickets, passport, some money, and pen and paper. I also never check my bags. Honestly, I can't recall if I checked a bag on that day in Dorval. Maybe I did. Most of the time, I travel with a small backpack that also converts to a suitcase. No, not much has changed, except for one thing: I do not wear a watch anymore. I haven't for the last twenty-six years.

The moment of departure is a particularly brief one if we are to consider the whole trajectory of the Traveler's journey, and even more so if we are looking at the long-term Travelers who are on the road for months or years at a time. The return home, also, represents a brief moment in time within the whole framework of the journey. Again, the parallel with man's life on earth is intriguing. The moment one is born and the moment one dies both occur instantly. Yet the significance of these moments is paramount. We understand that a man can prepare to die, but we seldom concede that a man can also prepare to be born. When we do, we are most likely referring to life after death or, for the religious minded, to eternal life after earthly death.

I believe that man does prepare for his birth to the same extent he can prepare for his death. I believe that life on earth is eternal. When we think of it, life cannot be anything but eternal, no matter when or where we ponder this issue or how we conceive of life. Life can never be constrained by mental conceptualizations, no matter how clever they are. Life simply is. Life is alive only in the now. When the imagination has roamed the full spectrum of life's countless departures and returns it comes to rest at the well of life, in the eternal now, the source of its power.

At any time the Traveler may choose to prepare to leave or prepare to return. He may want to spend a considerable amount of time and energy doing either or he may impulsively buy plane tickets, for instance, and board a plane that same day. Moreover, a Traveler may have prepared for months and years before the departure finally occurred, while a returning Traveler, especially if his travels were long term, can still be in the midst of dealing with important issues engendered by his return home. I like the term "reverse cultural shock" which was crafted by anthropologists to describe difficulties field workers experience in adapting back to their own culture after a prolonged absence studying the culture of another people. These issues are intricate. Some Travelers return home but are never truly at home anymore. Departing and returning, being born and dying, dawn and dusk, the flux and reflux of the tide; these are profound and evocative images that stir powerful sentiments from deep inside our beings. They speak of completeness, wholeness, and oneness. They point to cycles, unbroken circles and cellular memories of things that were, are, or will be. When one is born, one has to die. When the sun rises, it also has to set. When the tide comes rolling onto the shore it has to ebb again toward the ocean. When the Traveler leaves, he one day has to return. What happen in between these two crucial moments are a life, a day, and a journey. These cycles, natural rhythms of our existence, speak the common language of our humanity.

When the Traveler roams the world in harmony with his own natural rhythm, he is amplifying the natural rhythm of the world and adding his unique quality to its magnitude. His heart and the heart of the world beat as one. One's own beating heart, its steady pulse, is our innate connection with the natural world, with life beyond births and deaths, with each other, and with the tiniest drop of water in the vastest ocean. Our lives on earth, the elegance of one's destiny, whatever that may be, are intended to put us in touch with the rhythm of our own unique beating heart and to let it resonate through everything we do and for everyone to see. This is why it is so important for the Traveler to find his rhythm. Without it there is no journey.

Many Travelers I have interviewed used the word *journey* to describe their travels around the world. They also like the word *rhythm* when they express the idea of being tuned in to the travel mode and the sense of deep satisfaction it brings. They talk about "embarking on a journey" but none have spoken of ending the journey. The return home is perceived as another phase of the journey but not as the end of it. It's necessary to come back in order to leave again. There is no ending to the journey, only transformation. This makes sense because the learning that takes place during the journey is an ongoing process that lasts a lifetime. How could someone put a limit on learning? It also makes sense because a Traveler who has returned home is always preparing for another departure. How could a Traveler not want to travel?

There is much to do before the Traveler leaves. Or perhaps there is little to do. Much time is needed to prepare for the journey. Or, again, there may be no preparation time at all. The mere desire to leave may be enough preparation. The lure of the road and the promise of discoveries, both outwardly and inwardly, entice the Traveler to leave, to cross the threshold that separates the familiar world from the unfamiliar world. That threshold, at one time so clearly recognizable by all Travelers, is today an interior one that each Traveler has to identify and learn to cross over in order to begin the journey. This inner movement into the unknown may have an outward manifestation, such as crossing an ocean aboard a plane; nevertheless, its inception into the framework of the journey bursts out of the Traveler's inner landscape upon earth's landscape.

Any trip taken is a gift to be cherished. It doesn't matter where one goes or how long he travels. It doesn't matter why one moves from one place to another. The act of moving itself is enjoyable and exciting. Any trip becomes a journey when one's awareness is attuned to the rhythm of movement itself. There is an intense stillness in movement, just as there is profound silence in sound. It is in the center of this stillness that one's rhythm is to be found. As the Traveler uncovers it he is imparting meaning to the trip, to movement itself, to his life. He is on a journey. Socrates (c. 469–399 BC), one of the most influential classical Greek philosophers, is known to have said that a life left unexamined is a life not worth living. The Traveler may think of the journey as the life examined of which Socrates spoke, the one that is appreciated for the valuable lessons it teaches.

Imaginary and Real Journeys

I mentioned earlier that the first task of the Traveler is to find his rhythm. All the same, each journey possesses its own unique rhythm. One may wonder: Is there a journey awaiting the Traveler? Or is the Traveler fabricating his journey? In medieval times, when the young knight saddled his horse and rode alone toward the dense forest, he was praying that great adventures would soon visit him. His journey really began with the first battle. The journey had found him. He had risen to the occasion by doing battle and by proclaiming his identity to the enemy.

When Miguel de Cervantes' (1547–1616) character, Don Quixote de la Mancha, set out with his loyal squire Sancho Panza on his journey to fame and fortune, the framework of the knight's journey had already collapsed in late sixteenth-century Spanish society, even though the chivalrous romances were still broadly read. Keenly aware of the changing times (the first part of Don Quixote de la Mancha was published in 1605), Cervantes created an ironic hero in the personage of Don Quixote. Although beyond sound judgment and in spite of the overwhelming evidence far and near that the chivalrous universe was disintegrating, Quixote perseveres in living the great adventure of an accomplished knight. Don Quixote was no more a medieval knight. He had become a modern hero, one who becomes illustrious because he fabricates his own journey.

The journey has a natural rhythm to it and the duration of the journey is ultimately without importance. The awareness of the process is what matters. To recognize the natural rhythm of any journey is to feel our own heartbeat and, once tuned to its pulsation, a second, an hour, a day, or a year are all the same. Just as any single day in the life of an individual contains all the attributes of a lifetime, any movement (no matter how brief its duration) contains all the attributes of the journey and the passage it entails. A journey is based on movement, all kinds of movements, and on our capacity to convey awareness and meaning to it. When the Traveler is fully committed to the journey, there is no visible difference between the Traveler and the journey.

It is very common for returning Travelers to comment that in hindsight their overall trip possessed dreamlike qualities. Sensory associations instead of intellectual discourse better achieve the remembrance of the voyage. Dream events that took place during the trip now find a way to infiltrate the recollection of objective events. If someone gives an account of the trip his mind strains to block off the almost tangible pathway between the dream events and the objective happenings. However, if the same person is to give a sensible account of his journey, no such effort is necessary. Dreams and physical events are intertwined to give shape and meaning to the journey. This situation is a strong sign that the Traveler had found his rhythm.

A couple of months after the completion of a three-week trip with my father in Egypt and Israel, I heard him saying that it was hard to believe that the trip was not merely a dream. My father's journey had impressed itself on his life forever. French poet and filmmaker Jean Cocteau (1889–1963) wrote proficiently about the particular quality dreams assume while traveling. In his 1936 travel book *Mon Premier Voyage (Tour du monde en 80 jours)*, Cocteau writes about traveling in countries that are not mentioned on any maps. As his travels unfold, he becomes earnestly responsive to the imaginary characteristics of the factual trip. His poetic sensibility casts the Egyptian camel as a marine courier as he sails across the ocean to Cheops.

Poets, he explained, like to know, while tourists like to recognize. And it is clear that, for Cocteau, to know anything one has to flex one's imagination in many directions. I recall my own dream while riding a night bus from Cairo to Luxor along the Red Sea with the full moon gleaming on the shady waters and the bus driver periodically falling asleep at the wheel. I would invariably wake up in time to tap the driver's shoulder only to fall back asleep into my own underwater adventures. To this day, I still cannot separate the dream from objective reality. It seems to me that to do so would diminish the richness of the whole experience and lessen its educational value.

The Travelers I met during my fieldwork were often amazed that they were living their long-cherished dream of traveling around the world. "Sometimes, when I open my eyes in the morning," said Steven, a thirty-three-year-old American Traveler, "I take a long look at my room, wherever that might be, just to be sure that it's not a dream, that I'm really traveling all around the world. It's a great feeling. Sometimes I'm a little afraid it will disappear and I'll wake up in my bedroom back home."

Many Travelers also mentioned how their dreams seem to be different on the road, perhaps more real or closer to their conscious mind. This is how Ben, a young twenty-four-year-old Traveler from Holland, described it: "I would often dream of places I would see the following week. It's hard to explain. It's almost as if I was telling myself, in dreams, where to go, what to see or people to meet. I don't have those dreams when I'm not traveling. I learn even while sleeping."

The kind of knowledge Travelers seek is very personal and yet it reaches out into the world. It is real and yet it reaches into the imaginary world. The knowledge Travelers value the most is the knowledge of one's identity as it expresses itself in the outside world.

In the beautiful tale of real and imaginary travels told by Marco Polo to the Tartar emperor Kublai Khan in *Invisible Cities* (1972), storyteller Italo Calvino (1923–1985) has the aging Kublai doubting that the young Polo had the time to visit all the fantastic countries and cities he described to him in such generous detail. Polo explained to the great leader that as they converse in the palace garden he is also active in a mental space where he is "moving up a river green with crocodiles or counting the barrels of salted fish being lowered in the hold."

The intuitive Kublai agreed and pictures himself riding his horse "caked with sweat and blood, at the head of my army, conquering the lands you will have to describe . . ."

Polo goes on to suggest that perhaps the palace garden "exists only in the shadow of our lowered eyelids, and we have never stopped: you, from raising dust on the fields of battle; and I, from bargaining for sacks of pepper in distant bazaars." Then, talking about the possible realities lived or imagined by the Khan and himself, Polo concludes that, "It is our eyelids that separate them, but we cannot know which is inside and which outside."

The use of the imagination, that is, the capability to form a mental picture of something or a situation not yet perceivable by the senses, influences both the Traveler's dreams and the objective events he meets on his journey. Without the use of the imagination—and of projection, which is the belief that the mental picture can be materialized in space and time—the Traveler's adventures will likely be inconsequential. The matchless quality of the Traveler's imagination is what impresses the events he encounters with an incomparable flavor and meaning.

Even the most unexpected event carries a familiar air to someone experiencing it. This intimate air emanates from one's imagination. If it were otherwise, if events were forced onto us, we would be incapable of participating in them, perhaps even unable to perceive them. The journey unfolds as the Traveler moves about, images or symbols from the inside world coalescing with those of the outside world to form the ordinary and extraordinary events of any day on the road. Dreams and imaginative impressions act as mementos of what was, is or will be, imparting great strength to the purpose of the journey. A windmill may be a windmill or a formidable enemy to be vanquished.

My South Pacific travels were coming to an end, at least for the moment. The journey impels Travelers to move on to the next destination. However, as a Traveler, I have also learned to always keep alive in my consciousness the possibility of coming back to any destination I visit, at any time and for any reason, or for no reason at all. The day before my departure, Nyla and her cousin caught up with me at my favorite coffee shop. They wanted to invite me that night to a farewell party in my honor. I had kept my travel plans vague, sometimes mentioning the possibility of leaving the following week. The truth was that I, "the big man," did not want a farewell party, meaning that I did not want to foot the bill for a big party. I just couldn't afford it anymore. And how did they know I was leaving the next day?

"It's all arranged," said Nyla. "The party will be at my house tonight. We'll cook all day. We'll have music and dance all night. You only have to show up."

"I will." I was surprised and deeply moved by my friend's thoughtfulness and generosity.

The party was memorable. Nyla's family and friends, all the people I had invited at the restaurant, were there. There was live music played by excellent musicians who were also cousins or friends of my friend Nyla. The food was superb and we ate, drank, and danced all night long. My plane was leaving at 7:05 A.M. I had brought over my backpack, ready to go to the airport from Nyla's house. It was already 5:00 A.M. when I woke up, slowly picking myself up from the floor where a dozen of the guests had

fallen asleep. I tiptoed my way between the snoring bodies, then looked for Nyla but couldn't find her. I sat down
at the kitchen table and wrote a thank you note, then
stepped out onto the street. There was no taxi in sight. I
hastily walked down the hill hoping to cross a busy street
where I could find a taxi. No busy street, no taxi.

Could I walk to the airport, I thought to myself? This
idea triggered the memory of another departure, this time
from Kathmandu in Nepal when a strike and a protest
orchestrated by Maoist dissidents prevented taxis or any
kind of motorized vehicles from using the road leading
to the airport. I had resorted to hiring a bicycle rickshaw
and paying the driver extravagantly to take me to the
airport. It took almost an hour and a half for us to get
about two miles from the airport before we were stopped
by militants. In my mind and heart I was already on the
airplane; I knew that my time in Nepal had come to an
end. I argued my case, offered a little money, all to no
avail. Bribery seldom fails but it did this particular time.
I was surprised. As a Traveler, I have often used bribes to
get myself out of jams. I stepped out of the rickshaw and
walked the final two miles to the airport. My flight was
delayed by an hour and I was able to make it on time. I
did not intend to delay the journey. At least I wanted to
do all I could do to meet the timetable of my journey.

I felt exactly the same way early in the morning in
Nadi; I knew that it was time to leave. How far was the
Nadi airport from where I was? I didn't know and couldn't
tell what direction to take since I was not familiar with
this neighborhood. I certainly knew that I didn't have
time to walk. As my mind was occupied with finding a
solution, my legs had taken me to a busy street where I
saw two taxis. At 7:05 A.M. I boarded a plane to Auckland,

New Zealand. From above, the Fiji islands looked like tiny jewels the gods had discarded then lost all memory of their existence. I made a promise to the same Pacific gods not to forget them.

The Threshold: Where and When?

The journey starts with the crossing of the threshold. Travel is about movement, about crossing the threshold, and about the powerful relationship between time and space, which serves as measure for movement. We live in a fantastic age during which the logistics of the where and the when seem so simple: I want to be in Kathmandu next Friday by noon. We need only to look at a world map and a calendar to determine instantly where to be and when.

I am in awe when I think of Magellan's circumnavigation of the world. Fernão de Magalhães, Magellan (1480–1521), was a Portuguese explorer in the service of the Spanish crown. He sailed for almost three years, but even so he failed to complete the circle because of his ill-timed violent death in the Philippines. The first uninterrupted around the world circumnavigation was in fact completed by a little-known captain, Juan Sebastián Elcano (1476–1526), who brought home the Vittoria, the only one of the original five ships led by Magellan to return home to Seville in September 1522.

Nowadays I may fly nearly anywhere in the world in less than twenty-four hours. The remarkable thing, though, is that if you could go around the world now, in a jet, but instead see the landscape of Magellan's time, it would look very similar to today's landscape. But what today appear to be minor differences seen from the sky would represent huge breakthroughs to Magellan.

Certainly the Panama Canal that now connects the Atlantic and Pacific Oceans by way of the Caribbean Sea, or the Suez Canal that links the Mediterranean Sea with the Red Sea, would have greatly facilitated Magellan's voyage.

What appears as a straightforward relationship between space and time is really only a facade that travel often pokes tiny holes through. Travelers from past times struggled more with the notion of "where" than the notion of "when." They had time, plenty of time. Consider this: When the Renaissance Traveler left Europe and sailed to the New World, it took him weeks and months to reach his destination. To him, the ocean was the threshold, and the time spent crossing it impressed his spirit with the awe, terror and merit of the journey. The crossing of the outer threshold triggered the inner one. The "new place" beyond the ocean was not so much a location in space as it was a location in time. By the time he had reached his destination, weeks or months would have elapsed in the old world. Furthermore, the Renaissance Traveler had no means at his disposal to find out what had happened at home while he was traveling. He probably felt cut off from his homeland while acclimating himself to a new place. For all he knew, time had stopped in Europe. No wonder he often thought that these other places were set back in time. If the intent of the Renaissance Traveler was to physically explore the world in as thorough a manner as possible, the essence of his travels involved movement in time at least as much as, if not more than, movement in space. The threshold was located in space (the ocean) but it was the passage of time that played most keenly on his psyche. Since today's Traveler can be nearly anywhere in the world within twenty-four hours, less emphasis is put on time. It may also appear that where we go becomes more significant than how we get there and how much time is involved in getting there. How does this affect the Traveler's psyche? Are Travelers in danger of becoming tourists?

It is imperative that Travelers be aware that the threshold is no longer in the outer world. It is inside us. The inner threshold is the one that impacts the outer one, whatever that may be. The psychological journey is the catalyst for the physical journey. The journey of the present-day Traveler starts with an inner motion that is translated in the outer world as motion in space and time. The physical world that was explored by the Renaissance Traveler awaits the intimate touch of today's Traveler who will awaken it all over again. The world will respond to what is inside the Traveler. And it will be different every single time.

Ultimately, to ask where and then to ask when is to split our consciousness. We often like to think of geography as the academic discipline of the where and history as the academic discipline of the when. But actually we know that one cannot be separated from the other. We intuitively understand the relationship between where people live and how they live their lives through time. We also understand the effect of time on space. This is an old notion that is still with us today. It was present in the historical writing of Hecataeus of Miletus (c. 550–476 BC), who based his history on ethnographical data gathered during his wide travels. Contemporary philosopher Walter Kaufmann[7] (1921–1980) writes of time as the dimension of change and how we spatialize time to

---

7. Walter Kaufmann was a German-American philosopher and poet, as well as a scholar and translator of Nietzsche.

reflect change. Kaufmann finds the human concept of time to be the result of our reflection about change.

Centuries have pushed the limits of the where, and we are now slowly coming to the realization that the where is always here. Nowadays we are exploring the limits of when. Naturally, the ultimate limit of when is now. A language of tomorrow will have to invent a word combining where and when. The next great adventure may be to chart the limits of the here and now. Or has this exploration been going on for ages?

Why Travel?

My flight from Nadi took me to Auckland in New Zealand. Auckland and its surroundings reminded me of Québec. Great coffee shops, well planned beautified urban spaces, handsome green hilly pastures, tightly organized farms, excellent dairy products and, above all, a sense of social organization and public safety. After a short week in Auckland, I continued on to Sydney, Australia where I stayed for about ten days. I then boarded a flight bound for Bangkok. Bangkok is a sprawling city that is both confusing and engaging. It is miles away, spatially and psychologically, from Auckland or Montréal. I don't think one can fall in love with Bangkok, at least rarely at first sight, but the more time I spent in the city, the more I came to appreciate and love what it offers to its visitors: intrigue and romance in its intricate and confusing urban makeup. Bangkok is many things for many people, but Bangkok is never boring.

Love for a place, a city, or a secluded area is a powerful and complex emotion. The first days I spent in Bangkok made me uneasy. The sights, sounds, and smells fascinated me but I could not relax and open myself, as I thought I should, to the full sensual experience the city offers. Why I was holding back was incomprehensible to my rational mind. Why did I come all this way, so far away from my hometown of Sherbrooke, to be unreceptive to the bursting exotic experience of Bangkok? What was holding me back? Why travel if your mind, body, and soul remain unreachable? What was happening here?

The bus I was riding had not moved more than a couple of blocks in thirty minutes. I was confronted by the infamous Bangkok gridlock. I stepped off the bus to walk the rest of the way. The rest of the way was no way, really. I had planned to go to a market I had spotted the day before while riding the same bus. I knew more or less the direction to take and began walking steadily in that direction. Soon enough, I was lost. Since I didn't know the name of the market I couldn't ask for directions. I kept walking, slowing my pace somewhat and paying attention to my shifting environment. What happened next is unclear to me.

It began with a minor headache. Then my gait became slightly unbalanced. I kept on walking. Soon my vision blurred and the next thing I knew I was lying flat on my back in the middle of the sidewalk looking up at numerous pairs of eyes staring kindly at me. The gaze of all these strangers comforted me. Two young men helped me get back on my feet. I thanked each of them by looking straight into their eyes before I lowered my head and upper body while joining my hands together. They looked somewhat confused by my behavior and kept smiling broadly, probably to hide their puzzlement. I felt well but terribly tired and with a strong desire to sleep. Perhaps I had eaten too much but not had enough to drink.

I thought about the time I had slept seventeen straight hours after a long and tiresome trip to Kathmandu. I was drained, had a cold with a stiff neck and was running a fever. It was the Tibetan boy (many Nepalese hotels are run by Tibetans) from the reception desk of the hotel who woke me up by knocking on my door. He was worried that something bad had happened to me. He invited me downstairs for a delicious Tibetan breakfast that, he said, would fill me with positive energy. It was his kindness that energized me.

In Bangkok I saw the same unexpected kindness reflected in the eyes of my Thai benefactors. When I finally made it to my room I hurriedly undressed and went straight to bed. Sleep was blissful and dreamless. I strongly believe that deep sleep is the best medicine for many bodily and psychic ills. I woke up early the next day refreshed and with a new attitude toward Bangkok: I wouldn't waste one more minute feeling inadequate or uneasy in exploring the complex beauty of this city. Why have I traveled to Bangkok, I asked myself. It is certainly not to feel sorry for myself or to waste a unique opportunity to broaden my understanding of the world. I resolved to do everything I could to learn about the city. In the process, I did fall in love with Bangkok. The process is part of the journey.

Why do we travel? As a student and practitioner of ethnography during my graduate work I was advised to address the what and the how and to leave the why to philosophers, educators, and moralists. It is true that ethnographers are better equipped to describe what is going on and how it takes place rather than venturing into the uncertainties of the motivations behind the actions of people. Nonetheless, and in spite of the warnings, I was determined to take into consideration the intricate reasons behind the human desire to travel. I wanted to because I was asking myself the same question: Why do I travel?

I first turned to history for answers. History tells us that we are not the first human beings to travel. There is a rich tradition of travel in human history, and a quick survey uncovers an unbroken thread linking travelers of all kinds, from the mythical ancient journeyers such as Odysseus or Gilgamesh to the medieval pilgrim or knight, from the Renaissance travelers of the fourteenth to seventeenth centuries to the backpackers of the sixties and seventies and the mass tourism phenomenon of the late twentieth and early twenty-first centuries.

Then I turned to philosophy. Philosophy reminds us that travel is a potent, inexhaustible and elegant metaphor for life's journey. Artists, poets, philosophers, and mystics of all times and all places have explored travel's complex nature and have stroked its subtle chords hoping to make the synchronicity between the outside world and our inner being resonate within us. Eastern as well as Western Travelers have traveled the world while sitting still. Philosophers of both East and West have said it doesn't matter how you do it.

Finally, I turned to sociology. Sociology emphasizes the concept that the Traveler never stands alone. Socially, his worldview is part of the cultural baggage he carries with him wherever he goes. Yet, individually, he is one unique expression of an immemorial tradition of movement from the known to the unknown, from one's familiar place to another's unfamiliar one. His travels have impact. Spiritually, he is one adventurous being traveling the inside of the outside world.

But still the question remains: Why do we travel? Why do I travel? I needed to approach the question from another angle. Why are we seldom asked why we travel? Instead people ask how we liked a particular place. Why we went there instead of another place? Or why we did not like it? These questions are rather easy to answer. But to answer the question, Why do I travel? is not unlike resolving an apparently insoluble *koan* (paradox for Zen meditation). Many answers flash upon the mental screen. One after the other, each presents its truth. Over and over we carefully consider them, admire their cleverness, play with their implications, and finally find ourselves concluding . . . Yes, but is this all? Is this the ultimate answer?

One fine morning it at last becomes clear: There was never an answer because there was never a question to begin with. It was a trick, a mental acrobatic stunt that blinded us to the simple paradox that the process itself is all there is. Everything is part of the process. Asking questions, providing answers, doubting the latter, reformulating the former. The only reasonable answer to the question "Why travel?" is another question: "Why ask?"

"What is the source of the light?" a Buddhist student once asked his teacher.

"As long as there is light, why should we ask?" answered the teacher.

Is this not satori, the Zen understanding of sudden awakening, of enlightenment, by simply acknowledging the presence of the light? Satori is not an answer since there was no question to be answered. Such enlightenment is simply to wake up, not unlike waking up each morning, over and over again. Through travel, countless human beings have encountered the unknown, have initi-ated change and have perhaps become aware of the light.

Travel is about movement, and movement is about changes in perceptions relative to time and space. Time and space are what make our world tangible, apprehen-sible through our senses, and traveling represents a very sensually stimulating experience: to be somewhere else, at some other time. It is an irony of our senses that we know, as a child easily knows, that these other places and other times are with us, have always been with us, and always will be with us. Traveling is as much a question of expanding our being as it is taking the physical body to a different location.

Nevertheless, the sheer delight of deciding where and when to go and the materialization in time and space of this intention is a powerful accomplishment and a truly satisfying experience. Moreover, it mirrors our deep knowledge that we are what we concentrate on, that our thoughts, feelings and desires are physically visible and sensually experienced. With this in mind, we are not only traveling to one place at a given time but we are also remaining still and expanding our being across and beyond space and time. Thus, traveling the outside world serves as a metaphor for traveling the inside world. And the exploration of the inside world spills over into the outside world. The journey is always only beginning. And the learning is incessant. And the knowing is ever-present. And the delight is palpable. And the joy is con-tagious. This is exactly how I felt during my first taste of solo travel in Spain and Northern Morocco.

This was in 1976, one year after Franco's death. I remember being impressed by the political graffiti visible everywhere on the walls of public buildings and the eagerness of Spaniards to talk about politics. I had just turned seventeen. I had gone to Spain for four weeks, ostensibly to study Spanish. As I mentioned in Chapter 1, I did not study very long. I attended classes for two days and on the third day left with three friends to travel to Andalusia, Ceuta, and Morocco. I lost my main traveling friend on the ferry between Algeciras and Ceuta, looked for him for a day or two and then traveled with the other two friends for a few days before striking out on my own for the remaining time. I was reunited with my friend on the plane heading back to Montréal. We had bought our plane tickets together.

Traveling alone appealed to me immediately. It was very comfortable, yet adventurous. I quickly learned when to trust people and when to protect myself or even flee for my life. I was very young and naïve, yet traveling by myself for the first time taught me lessons I have never forgotten. I felt that I came back home a different person. The beautiful Andalusian cities of Sevilla, Granada, Córdoba, Málaga and, most of all, the city of Toledo left an indelible impression.

While in Spain, El Greco (1541–1614) became my favorite painter and remained so for many years afterwards. The emaciated bodies across the canvas are there only as clothes for the spirit and the dark but vivacious light that bathes his paintings seems to be coming from his own tormented soul. I like the story told about El Greco, about how he refused to open the windows of his house because he was afraid it might diminish the intensity of his own interior light.

I had read Ernest Hemingway's (1899–1961) *For Whom the Bell Tolls* and couldn't wait to see a corrida. I did not like it. I had listened to flamenco music before I bought a ticket in Sevilla to experience the real flamenco. That I loved. I became convinced that the striking leading dancer was looking straight into my eyes during the entire performance and I vehemently refused to believe that every man in the audience felt the same way. She was a remarkable performer.

I walked through the majestic Alhambra gardens built by the Nasrids in Granada and tried to picture life in al-Andalus (the Arabic name for Hispania or Iberia) in the fourteenth century. I was overwhelmed by the fresh sounds, scents, and ideas racing in my mind during a simple walk. Yet, at the same time, it felt very familiar, almost ordinary in some inexplicable way. This singular feeling became even stronger when I visited Toledo, a city that struck a deep chord inside me. An ancient Visigoth capital after the fall of the Roman Empire, then a Muslim stronghold until the Christian Reconquest in 1085, Toledo eventually emerged as the Christian intellectual capital of Europe where Arabic remained the language of culture and learning and its prosperous Arabo-Islamic legacy became an irresistible attraction to many Europeans.

Toledo's rich Islamic, Judaic, and Christian cultures came to play a pivotal role in the twelfth and thirteenth centuries by recording, translating, and transmitting the knowledge of the Greek, Persian, and Indian civilizations. Translators in Toledo continued the extraordinary work of cultural salvation initiated by the Abbasid caliphs of Baghdad between the eighth and tenth centuries when Greek learning was translated into Arabic. In Toledo, these manuscripts were made available in Greek, Latin, Hebrew, or Arabic and provided the bridge that linked the Greek world of 500 BC with that of al-Andalus and the later European Renaissance of 1500 AD.

Al-Andalus under the Umayyad rulers was an economic and cultural center of great renown. It began with the arrival of Abd al-Rahman in Cordóba in 755 and the battle he won to establish his governorship in May 756. The exiled al-Rahman had left his native land in Damascus, Syria after the Abbasids, a rival Muslim power, had defeated and massacred his family and the entire Umayyad dynasty except him.

Al-Andalus lost its predominant role in mixing and shaping cultures with the fall of Granada in 1492 when Spain expelled the Muslims and Jews who refused to convert to Christianity. This was the same year Christopher Columbus sailed west across the Atlantic. Some scholars believe that Columbus had been commissioned by the Jewish community in Spain to find a new home for them.

The story of the Jewish exodus from their home in Spain is exquisitely expressed in Sephardic songs and ballads dating from this period and originating with exiled Jews in North Africa and Asia Minor. Some of the most haunting lyrics and melodies came from Turkey. As the Spanish Jews continued to settle in their new countries of adoption, they composed gorgeous music expressing their deep longing for their true home, for al-Andalus, also called Sefarad. The Sephardic Jews have probably brought the traditional Spanish ballads to more peoples and places than the conquistadores. Perhaps some of the conquistadores themselves were conversos, Jews recently converted to Christianity. I love this music.

My personal affinities with Andalusia run deep and are strong. Cervantes, who I first read as a teenager, claimed that the story of Don Quixote de la Mancha was revealed to him by a book written in Arabic by an Arab historian, Cide Hamete Benengeli, which he said he had found in the old abandoned Jewish quarter of Toledo. I thought about Cervantes' dramatic flair and astute narrative skills when I first had the idea of writing this book. I also thought about the Toledo link and my attraction to the intermingling Jewish, Muslim, and Christian cultures of al-Andalus.

I kept a detailed journal of my travels in Spain and Morocco. In my 1976 notes I read that while shopping in Tangier, Morocco I only pretended to drink the mint tea that was kindly offered to me by merchants. I was afraid the tea might have been drugged. This occurred the day after I had inexplicably lost my traveling friend who had boarded the ferry with me but never got off the boat. Needless to say, I was suspicious of everything and everyone for a time. In Manila in 1994, after I had befriended a man posing as a professor of languages (he spoke French and English fluently as well as Spanish and Tagalog), and after I had spent a whole afternoon with him and two of his cousins, I accepted an invitation to go to his house to see his sixty-five-year-old aunt. His "lovely aunt."

I wasn't at all suspicious. We went there by buses and taxi. The aunt offered me a beer and that is all I remember. The drink contained the drug Rohypnol or something akin to it. This drug paralyzes the part of the brain that evaluates what is in one's interest to do or not to do without affecting body motion. Under its influence, one does exactly as told and remembers nothing of what happened. It is sometimes called the date rape drug. I was robbed and sent back to my hotel in a taxi. I had little money on me and some of it had to be used to pay for the taxi. I walked in the lobby of the hotel smiling and laughing. That is what I was told the next day by the manager of the hotel who told me he thought I was drunk.

I woke up the next morning with a massive headache and an off-balance gait. I read in my notes: "Been robbed by compassionate criminals, feel so vulnerable. Have all my body parts but still looking for missing parts every time I take a shower. My head is about to explode and I can barely walk straight. But what a magnificent day it is today!" It was indeed a soothing rainy day. Enough rain to wash away my disquiet.

To this day I often wonder what really happened. Had they only been after my money? If so, they must have been quite disappointed. And they even paid for the taxi to my hotel. Were they after my kidney and changed their mind at the last minute? Maybe one of the four pleaded my case to the others. The next days and weeks after the incident, I felt so lucky to be alive and intact. A young Japanese man who stayed at my hotel had worse luck. They took one of his kidneys and left him unconscious in a park where he was beaten and robbed of his clothes. These days, one of the best places to buy a kidney is in Moldova in Eastern Europe where some men and women voluntarily sell one of their own. Organ sellers in Moldova receive about $3,000 for a kidney.

About eight years after the Manila incident, I was having coffee at the Asturia, a restaurant on the Zócalo in Acapulco, catching the breeze from the Boca de China nearby. I was thinking of the Galeón de Manila that used to come through the Boca de China in January carrying goods from the Orient. Daydreaming, I studied the Malaysian features on the faces of some people walking through the Zócalo. I sighted a familiar silhouette swiftly passing by as if he were a ghost. Our eyes locked briefly. I spilled my coffee on the table, jolted by the revelation. He was gone as fast as he had appeared. Those were the eyes of the Manilan compassionate criminal. I ordered another coffee. I wanted to stay awake.

Advice to Would-Be Travelers

When you leave, plan to return; when you return, plan to leave. Always be aware of the journey.

$\backsim$ 3 $\backsim$

The Traveler

There was an incident in India during the first leg of my trip around the world, which months later unexpectedly triggered my interest in the historical figure of the Traveler. I was visiting a little-known archeological site in a desolated stretch of land in the Rajasthan countryside. As I was sitting on the broken steps of the remains of a religious temple I spotted a band of baboons in the vicinity. After a slow walk toward me, the chief baboon suddenly raised his right arm as he stared at me with disdain; he then lowered his arm, thus giving the attack signal to the other eleven baboons behind him. They made a run at me. I took off instantly, leaving behind my almost empty camera bag; fear was fueling my legs and I repeatedly screamed for help. I knew that at least one person, the guide I had hired for the day, could come to my rescue. And he did. After an interminable run, during which I kept screaming for help, he showed up armed with a long bamboo stick which he used to strike the ground constantly and loudly in front of the band of baboons. They finally dispersed.

"They are vicious," he said to me. "You are lucky. They would have bitten and scratched your skin deeply;

they don't like intruders. These ruins are their territory; you violated their territory."

"Why did you not tell me this earlier?"

"You never asked."

I had seen baboons many times before the incident in the Rajasthan. They always left me alone and I never paid too much attention to them. I had seen them going through the belongings of tourists and leaving with a thing or two. I knew they could be thieves. They now had my camera bag with the two lens filters in it. I had also seen them fighting with each other. But I had never been concerned about my safety while amongst them. This is no longer the case. After my flight for life I have paid very close attention to the behavior of baboons. I swore never again to be blind to the early signs of agitated or irritable baboons. While under attack, time stood still. How long did I run before help arrived? It could have been five seconds or fifteen minutes. I honestly have no idea. The moment was timeless.

Months later, in Thailand, the baboon incident came back to my mind. What actually flooded my mind was the intensity of the timeless moment I had experienced. The intensity was still fresh after all that time; at this particular moment, walking on the beach, I felt that my journey was timeless. The mind works in mysterious ways and I do not pretend to understand how it does what it does, but I learned long ago to pay attention to the mind when it insists on bringing back a past experience with such intensity. The timeless moment, I repeated to myself. What is timeless about it? I thought of a question Jack Huber[8] (dates unavailable), a student of Zen meditation,

---

8. Jack Huber. *Through an Eastern Window* (New York: St. Martin's Press, 1965).

asked after the completion of a trip around the world in the early 1960s. Perhaps he felt what I was feeling in Thailand. The question was: "How long is a moment?"

How long is my moment on the road, I was asking myself while walking on a deserted beach somewhere in the lovely South Islands of Thailand. Will I ever make it back home? What do Travelers do when they entertain the idea that they may never go back home? What am I supposed to do? What have other Travelers, in the distant or near past, done in my situation? I cannot be the first Traveler to ask himself these questions, can I? What about Jack Huber?

By the end of the day—and still walking—I came to the conclusion that the length of a moment for a Traveler was the length of the journey. And because the substance of the journey is awareness, the length of the journey is immeasurable in time and space; its meaning is conceivable only through awareness. It took me a whole day to figure this out. But what of other Travelers? What about my history as a Traveler? What is our history? I suddenly had a burning desire to find out more about my past. I needed that knowledge.

History of Travel

Our history, human history, is also the history of Travelers. Travel historian Eric J. Leed[9] (1942–) underlines a fundamental aspect of classical ancient travel when he demonstrates how gods or the almighty God decreed ancient travel. The journey of Odysseus was initiated, overseen and brought to a conclusion by divine intervention. Even the biblical story of Adam and Eve being expelled

---

9. Eric J. Leed, *The Mind of the Traveler: From Gilgamesh to Global Tourism* (New York: Basic Books, 1991).

from the Garden of Eden was God's decision, Leed points out. This forced departure inaugurated man's journey on earth. It illustrates the Judeo-Christian perspective on the beginning and the potential meanings of man's life on earth, one of them being to return to paradise. The original sin was the cause of the expulsion from paradise. Other religions have different stories to tell and varied insights to offer. The classical hero's struggles may well have been numerous and formidable, but he knew that he would never triumph if he did not seek first and obtain the favor of the gods or God. Without it, he was lost. Man himself sanctioned modern travel. The humanitarian undertakings of the Renaissance and Enlightenment eras substituted reason for God, the potency of the intellect for that of faith and the rationalization of the scientific enterprise for the holy might of the Church. The modern Traveler's authority came from his belief that he himself was the well of knowledge and the architect of his destiny, that the use of reason alone could unmask the mysteries of the universe, and the practical usage of scientific method could order the world in well-defined black-and-white categories: what could be scientifically proven and what could not.

While the ancient Traveler sought signs of his God or gods in the exterior world, the modern Traveler sought signs of his Reason. And each found what they were looking for; the heroic man always runs into that for which he is searching. After twenty years of aimless travel, Odysseus was finally able to come back home to Ithaca, to his beloved Penelope, with the help of the goddess Athena, daughter of Zeus, and Leucothea, a sea goddess who wrapped a veil about Odysseus to prevent him from drowning after a tempest wrought by Poseidon forced him to swim in turbulent waters for two days.

By contrast, when Captain Cook sailed to Tahiti to chart the transit of Venus during the first of his three remarkable voyages to the Pacific, he relied on new technology such as the chronometer to effectively plot a course throughout the vast spaces of the ocean. When his ships returned to England in 1780 without Captain Cook, who had been killed by natives on February 14, 1779 at Kealakekua Bay on the island of Owhyee (the Sandwich Islands, Hawaii), the major outlines of the Pacific Ocean and the world map had been drawn. This remarkable achievement brought to a conclusion the intrepid efforts of European explorers to map the lands and waters of the world beginning with Magellan's successful attempt to reach eastern Asia by sailing west (he too had been killed by natives, this time in the Philippines on April 27, 1521).

At last it appeared that the *ekumene*, an ancient Greek concept that refers to the inhabited Earth, had been thoroughly mapped by 1780. Cook's astonishing accomplishments launched the great era of scientific explorations committed to the investigation of the natural world, which was made understandable through reason, and the use of innovative and exciting scientific instruments. In 1797, when Alexander von Humboldt (1769–1859), the great Prussian geographer, naturalist, and explorer who traveled lengthily and made a significant contribution to the field of biogeography, prepared for his extensive travels in Europe, Russia, and the Americas, he assembled a vast array of instruments such as barometers and thermometers, a telescope, a chronometer, a balance, a eudiometer to study the gases in the atmosphere, a cyanometer to measure the blueness of the sky, and a sextant.

Today's Traveler is neither the ancient Traveler nor the modern Traveler. Or perhaps he is a little of each. The journal he often keeps is certainly a reminder of the scientific log any respectable eighteenth-century Traveler was asked to fill out daily. The latter was told that only observable events or phenomena that were written down had actually happened. He probably dreaded, as much as did the classical Traveler, an unfavorable turn of events during his journey. The only difference is that he may have blamed bad luck when the classical Traveler faulted the gods.

One of the things that I wanted to know at the beginning of my research on long-term Travelers was how we came to this extraordinary age of mass tourism that we take for granted today. In other words, what is the recorded history of organized forms of travel and of tourism? My research brought me to look closely at early records of travel for pleasure during the Roman Empire. Travel historians mentioned the fact that many wealthy Roman citizens took second homes in the Bay of Naples.

The upper classes of the ancient world often traveled for pleasure. Wealthy Romans took advantage of the extensive road system linking far-flung parts of the Empire to see the world. The most fortunate traveled in wheeled wagons down to the Bay of Naples, then on boats sailing the Adriatic heading east. They visited mainland Greece and the Aegean islands, Turkey and made their way down the Asia Minor coast to Upper and Lower Egypt and the borders of Ethiopia before heading back home. This circuit of the ancient world would become the blueprint for the eighteenth century "Grand Tour" of France, Italy, Greece, Asia Minor, and Egypt.

I was also attracted to the singular traveling figures of the Middle Ages, the pilgrim and the crusader. The pilgrim of the fifth century was an odd traveler in the early days of the Christianization of the Roman world but a very familiar figure by the eleventh century. The crusader's journey was also a form of pilgrimage, one that reclaimed by force sacred sites from Muslim occupation. The twelfth century would see the appearance of the knight who sought adventure and fame. He traveled by choice, on his horse, to express his freedom and to achieve social status. He welcomed and even sought out battles to make a name for himself.

Later on, the voyages of discovery and the scientific expeditions set out to discover new worlds for the glory of the mighty European powers. They also collected data in faraway worlds for the sake of knowledge and the advancement of science. The explorer of the sixteenth and seventeenth centuries collected exotic observations and tried to make sense of them within his socio-cultural framework. He wanted to rationalize the world and came to believe that superior technology equated to superior human beings. European culture was considered modern in comparison to the rest of the world. European man— not God—became the measure of all things.

During the Renaissance, the concept of traveling as a means to complete a well-rounded education, a notion also popular in ancient Rome, was very fashionable. The idea was for a well-educated young man to go see for himself what he had learned in books—the historical sources of knowledge. He was instructed to write down his observations in a journal. The farther one traveled meant the more knowledge one would obtain, and the whole world awaited the young European man eager to learn. This practice eventually grew into the Grand Tour of the young Englishman accompanied by his tutor. Truth was to be found out there in the world, in Greece and Italy or even in Egypt or India. By the seventeenth century, the European elites were traveling throughout Europe; by the eighteenth century, the Grand Tour was a well-established institution for privileged young men before they started their careers.

It was also during the Renaissance that the English aristocracy began to leave home annually for an English seaside resort. The first spas were built in the eighteenth century and became very popular all over Europe by the nineteenth century. The Industrial Revolution at the end of the eighteenth and early nineteenth centuries also provided faster and cheaper modes of transportation and fostered a new conceptualization of the relationship between work and leisure that encouraged travel for pleasure. The birth of mass tourism was just around the corner.

Thomas Cook (1808–1892), a Baptist minister in England, seized the opportunity provided by the new railway system to organize the first all-inclusive tour in 1842 and, in 1864, the first international tour to Egypt. He created the coupon system as a means for payment (the precursor of the traveler's check). He encouraged the standardization of hotels and restaurants and the expansion of the railway. As successful as Cook's Tours became, however, tourism on a global scale grew exponentially only in the second half of the twentieth century, especially after the introduction of commercial jet travel in 1952. Higher incomes, shorter work hours and longer holidays in combination with better transportation helped to convince million of individuals all over the world that travel is not only desirable, it is necessary.

Travelers, more than any other tourists, consider travel a necessity. It certainly feels like a necessity to me even though I'm well aware that it's really a privilege bestowed for the most part on citizens of the economically favored countries of the world. For that I feel lucky and am grateful. By positioning myself within the long and rich history of human travel, I become more aware of my social and personal identity as a Traveler as well as of the responsibilities it entails. This knowledge significantly enhances my travel experiences. For that, I feel empowered and humble.

Travelers of 1997–1999

It was my own personal travels that fueled a strong desire to find out about the experiences of other Travelers like me. The nature of travel and the experiences sought by Travelers became the topic of my Ph.D. dissertation. But who were the Travelers I studied in 1997–1999?

For the purpose of my research Travelers were defined in three separate domains: length of travel, mode of travel, and financial means to travel. In my research, to qualify as a Traveler, one had to satisfy all the following criteria: a) travel a minimum of three continuous months; b) be an independent and flexible traveler who organizes his or her travel schedule with an emphasis on informality and flexibility and who carries a backpack versus suitcases; c) be a low-budget traveler who, for the sake of extending his or her trip, chooses to live on a very limited budget.

I did a large part of my fieldwork in Guanajuato, Mexico. In some places, like Georgetown in Malaysia, Khao San Road in Bangkok, Koh Samui Island in

Thailand, Kathmandu's Thamel district, or Kuta Beach on the island of Bali, Traveler ghettos provide all the services needed. Extremely successful budget guidebooks have created these ghettos by directing Travelers there. In Mexico, Travelers do not have these ghettos, but Mexico is a very popular destination among Travelers. Other popular destinations in South America and Central America are Peru, Bolivia, and Guatemala. The most popular destinations are in Asia: Thailand, Indonesia, Malaysia, India, and Nepal. Laos and Vietnam have also become popular low-cost destinations for Travelers.

The colonial town of Guanajuato, Mexico, where I started my fieldwork research, is a more recent popular destination for Travelers. I chose this town because it receives rave reviews from all budget guidebooks and also because, being a bit out of the way, it does not see an invasion of international tourists or Travelers. Nonetheless, the flow is constant and considerable. Another major reason why I chose Guanajuato is Casa Kloster. I had been to Guanajuato twice before and knew about Casa Kloster and that it is always filled with Travelers. Moreover, when Travelers come to Guanajuato, most immediately enjoy the peaceful atmosphere and tend to relax. In other words, they are in a good disposition to talk about their travels. I met numerous Travelers there. I interviewed many of them and spent a considerable amount of time with many others. In the following section I recount what they told me.

Traveling Is Hard Work

If traveling provides an exhilarating sense of freedom and empowerment, it is also hard work. All the Travelers I talked to mentioned this in one way or another. Illnesses, bouts of loneliness and depression as well as the sheer exhaustion of the rigors of overland travel (long days and nights spent on sometimes very uncomfortable buses or trains) often take their toll on the body. Working hard at traveling is a rite of passage for most Travelers; it is the passage from aspiring Traveler to full-fledged Traveler.

Traveling the Traveler's way ought to be hard work. This dedication, this hard work, is one of the essential features that distinguish Travelers from other types of travelers or tourists. It is, therefore, understandable that Travelers insist on the hardship of traveling. For some, the meaning of the hardship of travel came into clear focus during a dramatic event on the road: "I was on this bus, in the state of Guerrero in Mexico, when masked gunmen came aboard and robbed us at gunpoint." (Hilda from Norway) For others, it happened more gradually during a period of intense soul searching on the road.

"I felt so exhausted, so tired of taking bus after bus, going on forever, always somewhere different. I started asking myself, 'Why am I doing this aimless traveling?' Then, one day, I froze; I could not take another bus. I just stayed in this small village for two weeks thinking about my life on the road." (Tim from Canada)

If each Traveler expresses the hardships of traveling differently, the important point is that all agreed that traveling is hard work. One seeks hardships in order to both affirm and confirm one's status as a Traveler. It represents an important rite of passage that makes an ordinary traveler or tourist a true Traveler. All Travelers have a specific anecdote or story to tell that marks this transition to full-fledged Traveler.

The very things that bring joy and freedom to Travelers are also what bring them anguish and insecurity. In other words, the joys and anguishes of traveling are made of the same material. John from the United States said it well: "The hardest thing when you travel is that there is no sense of place. Traveling is hard. You're by yourself. You make all the decisions. You don't know what bed you'll sleep in. . . . If I get a nice room, I just stay there for a week."

Travelers Are Not Tourists

The majority of Travelers abhor being called tourists. The dichotomy of tourist–Traveler is a significant concern among young Travelers, especially those who are just starting on their independent journeys. Most of them have had recent previous traveling experiences as a tourist, often with their families. It is therefore understandable that they want to separate themselves from their family touring past. Other older and/or more experienced Travelers recognize that even though they are Travelers most of the time, they are also tourists. Still, few Travelers will be caught photographing the sunset. Many understand, however, that for the local people they are tourists until proven otherwise. In other words, they have to prove themselves to the locals. They do this by spending longer periods of time with locals than regular tourists do, by making an effort to speak their language and better understand their socio-cultural values.

"Tourists are more interested in themselves, what they want or need. The people they meet are interesting as long as they get something from them," one female Australian Traveler told me. She continued: "Travelers are interested to learn about other people."

Most Travelers I talked to mentioned three main differences between Travelers and tourists: Travelers emphasize the importance of the journey (the act of travel itself), they make an effort to learn some words of the local language, and they embrace differences among cultures. Tourists emphasize destinations; they do not care about learning the local language and they often criticize or patronize the locals. Travelers and tourists who may be found at any point along the traveler/tourist continuum now increasingly use budget travel books, originally used almost exclusively by Travelers. As one Traveler put it, "The good news (about traveling) is that it is easier now. And the bad news is that it is easier now." Budget travel books are responsible for this. The best-kept traveling secrets are now published and available to millions.

Nowadays, Travelers and tourists alike share the same discursive touristic space. The subdivisions that differentiate the space are still important, probably more important than ever, but the overall picture is one in which tourists and Travelers increasingly have to learn to live together even though living separate lives. The ethnographic data, as well as my own reflections on the Traveler-tourist dichotomy, eventually led me to the conclusion that one of the main differences between the two is that Travelers come to ask questions related to their identities (personal and social): where and what is home and/or how is home defined or created? Tourists do not see the necessity of asking these questions. They want to experience a break from the monotony and rigors of work and daily life. They want to consume leisure and pleasant activities.

Being a tourist is a role we play mostly in groups. Many tourists (those who tour in organized groups), if left to themselves, will change their tourist behavior and revert to a more passive and contemplative role, such as simply observing the world going by. In other words, they become Travelers.

Travelers Want to Meet Locals

All Travelers I talked to had a lot to say about meeting locals. When asked why she travels, Norimi, a young Japanese Traveler, did not hesitate: "I travel to meet traditional people. In Japan everything the same. Same, same, always same! Except Okinawa."

Quite a few Travelers have found clever ways to meet the locals. One young Norwegian man I traveled with in the Pacific Islands, Urek, had a locally handmade harpoon that he carried with him. This always drew a crowd of locals around him. Urek would then ask them the best place to go harpoon fishing. He always met people who would take him fishing, and oftentimes ended up eating and spending time in their village. I always thought that he had found the best stratagem to meet people on their own terms. He met a beautiful local girl in this way (always high on male Travelers' list of most desirable things to happen).

Urek had been traveling for eight months when I first met him in Fiji. He was tall, slender, and blond. Many girls eyed him as we walked out of a small store where we bought a few things to cook that night. As we sped away on a motorcycle we had rented together, I could still see in the mirror one beautiful young woman who stood motionless by the door looking in our direction. Suddenly I saw a huge hand blocking that lovely vision. It was Urek's hand, waving at the girl.

Urek and I were sharing the cost of motorbike rental but, more and more, he needed the bike all night and for a large part of the day. And he wanted me as a passenger on the bike less and less. Urek and his young lover had to meet in secret. The girl's parents would never have approved of such a relationship. But on some evenings, when they were supposed to meet, the girl did not show up. She explained to Urek that sometimes she simply couldn't escape her family's scrutiny.

One evening, I heard the motorbike pulling up to the house where we rented rooms. It was Urek, coming back disappointed one more time that his girlfriend had not shown up. After discussing his situation for a while, we decided to go to a local dancing club. That evening Urek and I drank a lot. I left the club alone late at night. I slept on a beach near the club. We had met friends, and Urek planned on staying with them instead of going back to the house. I didn't see him for the next two days.

When I finally did see him again at a Swiss bar popular among expatriates, tourists, and Travelers, Urek was wearing a white turtleneck. That's odd, I thought to myself. Here we are in Fiji, a tropical climate, and my friend is sporting a turtleneck. What's wrong with him? I could sense his uneasiness even as I approached him to talk about the night at the dancing club. We shook hands.

"How are you doing?" I asked him. There was no answer. "Nice shirt," I commented. He laughed nervously.

He bought me a beer. We cheered. It was only then, as we drank the beer, that I began to pay closer attention to his neck, at least to the parts I could see. I saw the tips of red marks diving underneath his collar. Many, many of them.

"God, what happened to you?" I exclaimed.

He hesitated a moment, then said one word. "Hickeys." I put my hand on the collar of his shirt and pulled it out to see well. Urek's neck had many, many large deep hickeys all over it.

"I was drunk," he started explaining, "and there was this girl."

"Has your girlfriend seen this?" I asked.

"I haven't seen her since, you know . . . Here, that's how a girl marks her territory. Now my girlfriend or anyone else won't have anything to do with me." Urek was devastated. "How long do you think it takes to go away?"

Another excellent strategy to meet locals was one used by Louis, a Québécois in his late twenties, with whom I had traveled on the Mexican Pacific coast. Louis always carried his heavy climbing equipment. What was he going to climb, the locals wondered? This too was a great attention-gathering device and a clever way to engage locals.

Social Analysis of Travelers

Social analyses of tourists, who they are and their motivations to travel provide valuable insights into our societies. The Travelers I studied in 1997–1999 were almost exclusively from the economically privileged countries of the world, from Western Europe, North America, and a few other scattered Westernized countries such as Australia, New Zealand, Israel, Croatia, Japan, South Korea, and Taiwan. Some were from more recently affluent countries such as Brazil, Argentina, Spain, and Chile. These men and women, aged anywhere between seventeen and sixty-five years, travel alone but often pair up with other Travelers for a time. They do this for companionship and to share expenses. They travel on a budget.

Travelers are very critical of their home societies. They deplore the excessive materialism, consumerism, and the lack of a sense of community, of relatedness. They seek a more organic, holistic, and simpler life. They would like for their social identity to be defined more along the notion of who they are rather than the notion of what they have. They rebel against Western capitalist societies' goals and representation of power status (prestigious job, nice house, nice car, designer clothes, and impressive bank accounts). They strongly criticize the attitude of always wanting more and the notion that more is better. Yet, by traveling the world in airplanes, trains, and buses, and using ATM and credit cards, e-mail, and calling cards, they conform to the very consumer ethic they reject so strongly at home. In this sense, Travelers are international tourists. If they denounce the ideology of consumerism, they are nonetheless part of its culture by the very fact that they travel around the world, as consumers of the world through the tourist industry.

By being away from home for so long and by moving from place to place so frequently, they also are in a weak position to contribute to the development of that sense of community they denounce as lacking in their home societies. Furthermore, they go away in order to rediscover authentic values in places and among people who often seek to reap the benefits of what Travelers want to escape, materialism and consumerism. The framework of their journey is socially bound by the common desire of Travelers to experience their idealistic version of the traditional world.

Travelers are alarmed at the fast disappearing traditional world, where they have located most of the values they feel are lacking in their own societies. Yet, their main challenge becomes clear: how to be a Traveler, as opposed to being a tourist, in a world thoroughly touristic. On the other hand, individuals from the "traditional world" are concerned that they are missing out on the beneficial values of the Travelers' home societies. Misunderstandings between Travelers and the Other are commonplace.

Travelers, more than any other type of tourist, consider themselves to be citizens of a wider, interconnected, intercultural world. As independent travelers, they incarnate the latest and hybrid philosophical contemporary version of the eighteenth-century European Grand Tour. Their travel experiences are valued for their educative, philosophical, and recreational as well as spiritual, self-transforming benefits. Travelers seek transformations in new and exotic environments, in places and among people as different as possible from what one knows. In their search for ever newer and more exotic environments, Travelers are constantly shifting, trying on new identities.

Their long travels to virtually every corner of the world say much about our lives at home. Their search for the Other points up their desire to understand themselves, the world they live in and their place in a highly structured and thoroughly touristified world that is constantly changing. They take pride in their world experiences and their self-identification of worldliness. Usually being affluent and economically privileged individuals in their own societies, they often seek in less-privileged societies the experience of having little or near nothing. Traveling alone with only a backpack is a good metaphor for this desire to strip oneself of what many Travelers perceive as the unnecessary personal, economic, or social baggage one usually has back home. Some even "go native" in an effort to understand what it feels like to be the Other or their perception of the Other.

If the lives of the Other seem attractive to Travelers, it is often because of the drastic contrast they represent when compared to their lives back home. The greater the difference, the more valued the experience. Travelers often perceive the lives of the Other as more simple and more communitarian. They think of their lives at home as more complicated, somewhat alienating and confusing. The hard lives of the Other, in the minds of many Travelers, are often estimated as being more satisfying and more meaningful than their own complex and often confusing lives at home.

They travel for prolonged periods of time, ranging from a few months to a few years. They follow a relatively standard itinerary, a contemporary updated version of the eighteenth-century European Grand Tour. Travelers are found all over the world, but especially where their tourist dollars go a long way. The travel circuits they tread are forged out of the trails blazed by the backpackers of the sixties and seventies, including the seventies Asia Overland Road and its eighties Asia Road version, or the Gringo Trail in the Americas.

Travelers' personal and creative journeys are well embedded in the social complexities and dilemmas of our societies. They denounce the lack of authenticity in our modern lives. Is the lifestyle of modern prosperous societies leading to loneliness and alienation? The Dalai Lama once made an excellent point discussing this topic. He explained that all over the world we find diseases that correspond to the particular environment, both physical and social, of a particular society. Consequently, we have stress-related diseases in urban postindustrial societies and diseases related to poor sanitation in developing societies.

The Bond of Travel

The Travelers I have interviewed shared what is often referred to as "the bond of travel." I have already pointed out some of the markers that stand for this bond. One of them is the crossing of the threshold. Another one is the experience of "hitting rock bottom" or "hitting a wall." As I mentioned, hitting rock bottom is a defining experience for the Traveler. What is particularly interesting is that it never fails to occur during the third or fourth month on the road.

For social scientists, these markers indicate that the social trajectory of the Traveler may conceivably be spelled out and that fresh insights into the nature of our societies may be generated from the study of its model. Yet the inscrutability of our true nature, of human nature, is the wonder of our lives on earth. The mystery is why we are alive. It is the miracle.

Hitting rock bottom away from home can be a traumatic event for some Travelers. It is the Traveler's dark night of the soul. Many decide at this point to go back home. Others, after going through a traumatic period, are ready to continue on their journey with a renewed sense of purpose. Some, though visibly shaken, genuinely find their rhythm as they emerge from the experience. This ordeal is an initiation into the society of Travelers. It is during this trying period, which may last a few days to a few weeks, that the Traveler takes a pragmatic look at who he is as an individual and as a member of a larger community, and what his purpose is in traveling the world. The intensity of self-analysis varies, naturally, from one individual to another. For those who choose to continue on their journey, there will be other such periods of intense self-reflection.

The process of thinking through one's own situation, difficulties or challenges is, honestly, an ongoing process. The efforts employed in comprehending our actions can only lead us, at best, to a fragmentary understanding of why we do what we do. The reasons are always very intricate, weaving human yearnings of self-expression and an unquenchable curiosity with an inherent sense of self-worth and an all-encompassing craving for social approval. Social theory, psychological examination or philosophical speculation illuminate various aspects of our capacity for action, but none, not even all the theories combined, irrespective of their ideological affiliations, can come close to a comprehensive and holistic understanding of why we do what we do.

I believe that even God, in all his compassion, or because of his compassion, when he becomes man, thinks and feels like man—because surely God can become whomever he chooses to be—cannot comprehend the totality of man's destiny. Moreover, I truly hope that man's destiny is a work of art, a graceful attempt at expressing the immeasurable depths of our existence. Before anything, or after everything, we exist. Only the particular expression of our existence is within boundaries, but its essence is perfectly free.

When the Traveler hits rock bottom, he becomes engaged in the process of self-analysis and will try to understand this physical, emotional, and mental ordeal from a number of different perspectives. Each Traveler will deal with it in his own way. However, the crisis yields unexpected dividends for one who sees it through. During the ordeal, when the Traveler asks himself what he is doing away from home for so long, he begins to recognize the tangled connections his thoughts, feelings, and beliefs have with his actions. Was he running away from some inextricable problem at home? How does this problem appear to him now that he is not home anymore? What does he think will happen when he goes back home: Will the problem still be the same? What does he believe to be the main benefits of his trip? Does he think of himself as being on a journey? If so, what does he think is the nature of his journey?

When Travelers recount their experience of hitting a wall during an interview, tears frequently come down their cheeks. I feel like a confessor. One young Catholic woman from Spain said that she considered me a priest and that she felt relieved to have confided in me. All I did was to listen. But to listen means a lot to someone who tells something confidential for the first time. Most of the Travelers I interviewed said that they have never told anyone what they had just said to me. The reason was simply because they believed no one would take the time to listen to something so intimate.

People, they believe, will avidly listen to someone's travel stories, the surface story of unusual or extraordinary events. But no one, except close friends or family, is interested in listening to the inner side of the story. Furthermore, it is often easier to confide in a stranger than in someone we know well. Travelers suffer from their inability to tell "the real story" to others. The real story is always personal and involves the whole being of the Traveler. The real story is that of the journey, not merely the tip of the iceberg (the trip).

There comes a time in a person's life when the difficulties or challenges intrinsic to the personal and custom-made nature of the life journey are out there, in the open, for all to see, or so it seems. For what looks like total exposure to the whole world is truthfully a show put up by one's innermost thoughts, feelings and beliefs to entice one's notice, to compel an individual to pay attention to the purpose of his own personal journey. Spanish mystic and poet St. John of the Cross (1542–1591) welcomed the arrival of the dark night of the soul as a positive experience that brings knowledge of oneself.

It is an opportunity for transformation, perhaps for a new beginning or a continuation with a rekindled sense of purpose. It is a boon disguised as confusion, a loss, a lack of perspective or drive to act. A tragic accident, the loss of a loved one, a prolonged illness, financial collapse, each can play the role of the transformer in someone's life. It is a pause in one's life, a moment of self-reflection that was built into the fabric of the journey itself from the moment one was born, or perhaps before. There may be one or several such times in a person's life. However, one of these events usually stands out as the great tremor that changes everything. The number of crises actually matters very little. What does matter is how one perceives the crisis and its purpose in his life. For the Traveler, it is also a time of remembrance. What if I return home now? Will it be as it was before I left? Where or what is home?

What Is Home?

A few Travelers I encountered on the road planned never to return home. I have talked to and interviewed one Traveler who claimed to have been traveling nonstop for nine years and another for twelve years. The fundamental terminology of the journey, with its departure, the travel experiences away from home, and then the return, refers to an innate language that is as familiar to man as blood running through his veins. The language of the journey is symbolic and its cardinal symbols are like doors to be opened and thresholds to be crossed in order to take in new sights. The return home is such a door; some Travelers cross it symbolically and do not see the necessity of physically returning home.

In today's interconnected world, it makes sense that the farther one travels, the closer one feels to home. The Traveler comes full circle. It may be because the Traveler sees in the Other what is missing from home. Or it may be that the Traveler sees too much of himself in the Other. But home is the point of comparison. Home is always with us. Or it may be that our complex lives beg us to rethink our conception of home. What is home?

Seasoned Travelers may tell us that the whole world is their home. The image is appealing, but it is a cliché. However, clichés are constructed from popular beliefs held over a long period of time. They are what many people at least once thought to be valid information. One of the most popular contemporary historical-travel authors, James Michener (1907–1997), chose the title *The World Is My Home* (1992) for his autobiography. He, and many others, may be right in thinking so because home is who they are and are becoming. One can never leave for anywhere without bringing oneself along.

Abroad, home is expanding. Back home, it is consolidating. This is a delicate balance, one created by a very unique state of mind. What one leaves at home when going away is the extra luggage, the things one does not really need for the trip in order to be oneself. That may be the attractiveness of travel. The essential things, good or bad, always remain with the Traveler. These are the values, key concepts or ideals that will be confronted by the Other's values, key concepts or ideals in an effort to expand one's horizons, to expand one's home.

On the road, life is made simple. One needs to go abroad to expand one's concept of home. Tourist enclaves give you back the extra luggage you thought you had left home. Everyone knows that the Hiltons and MacDonald's of the world are all the same. They are us. They are who we think we are when back home. They are comforting, homey, like an extra blanket from home special-delivered while you're traveling.

The concept of home is, without a doubt, central to Travelers who feel most at home in movement itself. That is possibly why they do not stay long in one place; they become homesick. I once had an interesting discussion with one of my students; he was the director of a city program to assist the homeless in New Orleans. We were in Québec City studying urban issues in Canada. In the evening we talked about my research on long-term Travelers and I was describing the sense of rootlessness Travelers experience and their yearning to belong and contribute to a community. What I was describing, he immediately pointed out, is how the homeless person feels.

Advice to Would-Be Travelers

Think of home as being who you are. You can never leave home.

4

The Other

I checked in at the Ayutthaya Guest House in Ayutthaya. As often happens in the life of Travelers, I had
come to Ayutthaya for a couple of days with the goal of
exploring the main sights of the former capital of Siam
(Thailand). I stayed two weeks and ended up coming
back on two separate occasions. The reasons for staying longer and coming back were Kook, Jane, Nui, and
Melissa; especially Kook and Jane. While having breakfast at the Guest House on my first day in Ayutthaya, I
met Kook and Jane, both wearing school uniforms. It was
Kook who first approached me.

"We are students of English," she said deliberately
with a slight British accent. "Do you speak English?"

"I do," I answered, "but French is my native language."

"I want to learn French too, but after I speak English
well. Would you care to join us for breakfast? My friends
and me . . . and I would like to speak English with you.
We have English class in one hour."

"It would be my pleasure."

Thus began my friendship with Kook, Jane, Nui,
and Melissa, my Thai sisters from Ayutthaya. Kook was
twenty-six years old and had one older sister who was

getting married the following week. She also had a boy-friend to whom she had been engaged for at least three years. She constantly complained about him but said that she would probably marry him in about four or five years. I sometimes doubted that he existed because he was never around. I did meet him later on at Kook's sister's wedding.

Kook is ethnic Chinese; both her parents are college professors of psychology. She was an A student and a natural leader. She was pretty, had a sturdy but well-proportioned body, mid-length black hair and soft eyes. She often said she wished she were more beautiful like her sister or Jane, but Kook's attractiveness rested largely in her unassuming manner in relating to others, especially men. She had a way of making you feel at ease.

Jane, on the other hand, was shy. She had cascading black curly hair, wide dark eyes, full lips, and an appealing smile, all very attractive features to men like me, solo Travelers. But Jane didn't like that much attention. She was very engaging on a one-to-one basis once she had gained your trust. Otherwise, she would rather recede to the background, discreet but attentive to everything, preferring to let her outgoing friend Kook take the lead. It wasn't difficult to fall in love with Jane, and I probably did, as did many other Travelers.

It was a Traveler from Norway who eventually won Jane's affection. They met during my last visit to Ayutthaya. I barely saw her then and I asked Kook why.

"She has a boyfriend. She likes him a lot. She will go to Norway to visit him in two months."

I once asked Jane why she didn't have a boyfriend. She replied that her boyfriend was not born yet. He was "born" a few months later. Jane went on to marry her Norwegian boyfriend. I received an invitation to the wedding in Norway about a year later. I wonder how she adapted to living in a cold climate.

Nui was a petite lively woman who spoke more with her eyes than with words. When I met her she already had a boyfriend, a handsome young English soccer player. Nui was in love, really in love, and one could tell, just by looking at her eyes and demeanor, that her love was the all-consuming factor in her life. She was ecstatic, then worried, jubilant, and then apprehensive. She wanted to marry her summer love but Nyle, the Englishman, wanted more than anything else to go on with his travels. Nui couldn't concentrate on her studies—or anything else for that matter—while Nyle, so it seemed to me, could concentrate on everything else but her. At one point, Nui thought she was pregnant. Nyle was shocked. It turned out that she wasn't.

Some of us staying at the Guest House played soccer in the municipal league. Nyle was the star player. One day after a game he told me he was going to leave in a couple of days.

"Please don't tell Nui. I have to leave now before she does get pregnant. Her love suffocates me. I can't take it anymore."

"You're not going to tell her anything?"

"No, I'll leave a letter."

"Yeah, perhaps that's better," I joked. "That way, she won't be able to castrate you!"

"Yeah, she probably could," he replied without any humor in his voice, perhaps remembering stories we had both heard about over-possessive Thai women. "She is the type, isn't she?" he asked.

I fell silent. Nyle left two days later. Nui cried for at least eight days, which was the number of days I stayed at the Guest House after Nyle's departure. By then, Nui had set a new goal for herself: to learn to write in English in order to communicate with Nyle. Unlike Kook and Jane, Nui did not like to study, but her motivation was so strong I never doubted her success. She even wanted private lessons but had no money to pay for them. Unlike Kook and Jane's parents, Nui's were not well-off. Will I give her private lessons? Could I help her understand Nyle's letter? What did he mean by signing off his letter with "Love always, Nyle"?

I, too, was ready to leave. Travelers are always ready to leave.

Melissa was the Thai sister I knew the least. I say "sister" because this is how they referred to themselves in communications with me. They always signed off cards and letters with "Your sisters." Or, when we talked on the phone, Kook (the spokesperson of the group) would say, "This is your sister Kook." Melissa, too, had a boyfriend, but I never met him. She was very busy and sometimes couldn't be with the four of us (me and my three other sisters). She was outspoken, always in a hurry and quick to laugh. She once asked me why I was not dating Jane.

"But Jane is my sister," I said. "That would be incest, don't you think so?"

"I don't understand the word incest."

"Sister and brother don't marry," I explained.

"I understand," replied Melissa.

I have to say that having sisters instead of potential girlfriends made things a good deal easier for me. Was it Kook who came up with this idea? I wouldn't be surprised. Kook is a very smart girl.

Spending a lot of time with my newfound sisters was very educational and comfortable. Friendship is about learning: learning about the other and about ourselves through the other. This process is even more transparent in cross-cultural friendships when differences seem more palpable than similarities. During side trips together, and simply by being with them, they taught me a lot about Thai culture. We often ate together. Although I very much enjoyed the animated meals I was accustomed to having with friends and family back home, with plenty of wine and everybody talking at the same time, I particularly treasured the peaceful, almost meditative mood of meals taken with my Thai sisters. Few words were exchanged, appreciation was given to each food tasted, especially to rice, which was always eaten first in gratitude for the most basic and nourishing of food in Thai culture. My sisters were also learning from me.

"Why can't I travel like you do, around the world and by myself?" asked Jane.

The question was not directed to me but to herself and to Kook, who had just joined us.

"In Thailand," Jane went on, "we only travel to see family. You don't go places where you have no family. If I do, nobody will understand what I am doing." She paused for a moment. "And I wished I were my brother. He can do more things like that, travel for no reason, and my family doesn't ask too many questions. But they will ask some questions. And you, you go wherever you want and nobody asks you why."

I agreed. But my issue, I thought, was that it is I who ask myself the question "Why travel?" We definitely had different perspectives.

My introduction to Thai society was mediated largely through Kook and Jane. They instilled in me a deep appreciation for their opulent and profoundly nuanced culture and my foray into that culture was enriched by our friendship. I felt very fortunate to have met them. The day I left, my Thai sisters gave me a silk shirt made in Thailand and a silver ring displaying the image of the Buddha. There was also a card that read: "The shirt is to remember us and our friendship; the ring is to protect you during the rest of your trip. Don't forget us, we will not forget you. We have memories together." I still have the shirt and I wore the ring throughout the rest of my journey. I have not forgotten them.

It is not easy to conceptualize the realities of other peoples. Not so long ago, most people different from us were either living far away from us or living quasi incognito amongst us. The "us" or "we" could have been anybody. Anyone thinking about other peoples positioned himself and those like him (his cultural group) as the "us" or "we" in contrast to "other peoples." They were other peoples precisely because they were not us. They were other peoples in other places—if not other times— living other lives. Until recently, it was relatively simple to conceptualize us and to use that standard as a measuring stick to understand the Other. In return, our understanding of the Other, however biased, influenced what we thought of ourselves. It has often been said that the European explorations were not about discovering other peoples but about Europeans explaining themselves to themselves by using the Other as a measuring stick.

Today it is no longer that simple. Even those spatially close to us may be socially and culturally a world apart. And others living far away may be socially and culturally very similar to us. The social and spatial realms of culture are an intricate mix, and this intermingling of the two often brings bewilderment. The physical world has in a way become much smaller, but in another way much vaster. This situation represents a challenge for the Traveler. It is also a source of puzzlement. The Traveler aspires to meet the Other. The more dissimilar socially and culturally the Other appears to be, the more satisfaction the Traveler seems to derive from the encounter. At the same time, he doesn't like being told that his neighbor back home may be the apex of his conceptualization of the Other.

When we think of it, there is only one "me" in the entire world; the other seven billion people are all "others." I can only recognize the Other one at a time and my knowledge of him or her is always mediated through me. There is no understanding of the Other who is out there for everyone else to see. Knowledge about the Other is always my personal understanding of who this Other is. Perhaps the appeal and the repulsion, the familiarity and inscrutability of the Other, is the mystery of self. Maybe opening up one's mind and heart to the Other is also opening up one's mind and heart to oneself.

Friendship and Tolerance

How can I understand someone different from me? There is a Chinese proverb that goes something along these lines: "Tell me, I will forget. Show me, I may remember. But involve me and I will understand." Travelers want to become involved. One of the greatest joys of traveling is to meet the Other. In hands-on travel encounters, this abstract Other becomes a flesh and blood person. A Traveler can only meet one person at a time, and time and good will are required to get to know anybody. Friendship is ecumenical.

For all the idiosyncrasies of each friend, for all the misunderstandings bound to ensue when two worldviews intermingle, the friendship is sanctified since it represents a desire to change simply because of the presence of the other person. Travelers value friendships developed with persons culturally different from themselves. They do so because they see in those friendships the opportunity for tremendous learning. Seasoned Travelers are also aware of the difficulties involved in building and maintaining those friendships and value them even more for that reason.

How could the Traveler be a friend to someone he meets away from home? First of all, he has to constantly remind himself that while he is not home, the other person is. I always thought that to travel the world lightly and joyously one has but a few rules to keep in mind: Always be exceedingly polite, observe attentively, reserve judgment, and smile a lot. Passports and visas may allow anyone to legally cross state lines and visit the wonders of the world, but they give nobody access to anyone's heart. Only unaffected human qualities such as patience and goodwill do that.

The Traveler's life is immensely enriched by friendships that begin while away from home. My Thai sisters spoke of building memories together. Fresh sights, sounds, and smells are now part of a Traveler's expanded life; it is as if they had detached themselves from a new friend's environment to become part of him. Individual, social, and cosmogonist conceptualizations that make up his friend's life circumstances and convey meaning to his daily life now also find refuge in his own mind and heart. In time, the Traveler can even consider his own culture from the point of view of his friend's culture, reflecting on it from the outside in, momentarily suspending allegiance to his cultural set, an accomplishment that was unavailable to him prior to his travel friendships.

New ideas, as well as foreign concepts, can be tried on as one may try on new or foreign clothes. Just as it is exciting to put on foreign clothes in foreign cultures or at home (even though one may wish to wear them in their home only), entertaining foreign ideas or new social concepts either abroad or at home is also stimulating. How does it feel to live with this concept of the extended family? a Traveler may ask himself while abroad. Or, how does it agree or disagree with my own culture? However, the key question is simple: Could I, even for a moment, perceive the world through my friend's understanding of his daily reality? One may argue that this is impossible. Or one may argue, as did the great sixteenth-century essayist Michel de Montaigne (1533–1592), that every man has within himself the entire human condition. In any case, the very attempt to comprehend someone else's day-to-day reality carries its own reward, that of tolerance.

The word *tolerance* is one of my favorites in any of the approximately six thousand languages presently spoken on earth. I don't know anything about those languages except for a handful, but I can hardly imagine a human language without a word to represent the concept of tolerance. Even in small and closed societies that not too long ago existed in isolation from the rest of the world, places such as the island of Papua, New Guinea or along the Amazon River in South America, I'm convinced that they too had a word that stood for the concept of tolerance. Even in a small culturally homogeneous group, there will always be individuals who choose to assert their idiosyncrasies in spite of, or because of, social disapproval.

How do society and the individual deal with this situation? Even if there were no word for tolerance, the idea of it has to exist in order to measure the scope of a disapproved individual's offense.

Tolerance implies diversity. It demands forgiveness, empathy, and patience. It generates compassion. It praises the individual's imagination, resilience, and creativity. Because the difference in the Other is often colorful, loud, and even disturbing, tolerance never comes easy. The Standard English definitions of the word tolerance include a) the capacity to endure pain or hardship and b) the sympathy or indulgence for beliefs or practices different from or conflicting with one's own. I particularly like yet another definition of tolerance: the act of allowing something. I like this last one best because it emphasizes the importance of letting the Other be who he is. There is no doubt that to observe a situation that is foreign to us, yet to deliberately withhold judgment, is a highly difficult task. However, if we do not withhold judgment, more than likely we will use the wrong measuring stick—our own personal and social values—to try to understand what we are witnessing. In this case, to be patient is to be tolerant.

My own definition of tolerance is one that recognizes the basic oneness of the human species and the interdependent nature of reality. Tibetan Buddhism speaks of this as the interconnectedness of all life manifestations. French philosopher and mystic Pierre Teilhard de Chardin (1881–1955) said it beautifully: "We are one, after all, you and I, together we suffer, together we exist, and forever will recreate each other." To be tolerant, in my own understanding of it, is to recognize the unlimited human potential in the other as well as in oneself and to acknowledge the complementarity and complicity of all human expression. The true Traveler cannot journey far without being tolerant. Yes, he may travel far and wide and for a long period of time; however, as far as the journey is concerned, without tolerance he will be like a captured animal endlessly pacing back and forth in his cage. To be tolerant opens the heart, and when the heart is open a single step forward is a whole journey.

We were sitting at a small beach restaurant just outside Malacca. We were there to savor a popular local dish called *laksa lemak*. It consists of noodles and prawns as well as other ingredients stirred in a rich (*lemak*) spicy curried (*laksa*) coconut soup. It was early evening and the numerous empty tables sprinkled on the beach were starting to fill up.

"We came on time," said Roland as he drew a cigarette from a full pack. "This is a very popular place and soon all the tables will be taken. They make the best *laksa lemak* in Malacca."

Roland, my Chinese Malaysian friend, and I had an agreement. He would take me around town on his motorbike to sample some of the best local gastronomy and I would foot the bill. This was our third culinary excursion into Chinese, Malaysian, and Peranakan cuisine. Roland belongs to the wide and vibrant culture of the Chinese Diaspora, but when asked what he is, he says Malaysian. He has never been to China but speaks both Mandarin and Cantonese Chinese. His everyday language is Bahasa Malaysia but he also uses English on a regular basis. He watches Chinese, Malaysian, and English-speaking television. He is a converted Christian and attends church every Sunday, but he also prays at the Buddhist-Taoist

Chinese temple near his house where the ashes of his ancestors are kept. In Roland's house a picture of Jesus hangs above a statue of Buddha. His hobby and passion is to meet foreigners and show them around town. By profession he is an accountant at the local private golf club though he doesn't like golf. Roland lives by himself in a spacious historic house.

After he ordered for us and finished his cigarette, Roland turned his attention to me.

"How is it to have sex?" he casually asked.

It's true that eating and sex are two basic needs and that talking about or indulging in one can lead to the other, but still I thought I hadn't understood his question.

"What do you mean, Roland?"

"Well, how does it feel to have sex with a lady?"

Is Roland gay? I wondered. I chose to confront him right away.

"Roland, you've only had sex with men?"

He laughed. "No, that is not what I mean. I never had sex with a woman or with a man. I am not attracted to men, but how is it to have sex with a woman?"

I was stunned. Roland was probably in his mid to late thirties and he had never ever had sex! His question was genuine: he wanted to know.

The drinks and appetizers came. We cheered up as we took a few sips of our Tiger beer (brewed in Singapore) and started chewing on the marinated and charcoaled pork and mutton served on thin bamboo sticks.

"This is the best satay I ever had," I told Roland, "and the peanut sauce is so tasty, and these rice squares, what are they? It's delicious."

"Yes, it is delicious; it's called *ketupat*. It's rice cooked in coconut leaf casings mixed with tripe and intestines."

I suddenly became more interested in the conversation about sex than minute details on the nature of my tasty food. Was it conceivable that a perfectly healthy human being who had taken no vow to remain chaste could have no interest in sexual activity?

"Roland, did you ever want to have sex with a woman?"

"Yes, but having sex complicates the relationship a lot, doesn't it? You have to get married or you have some kind of obligations toward the woman you have sex with. Don't you?"

He had a very good point. "But what about sex for money?" I countered. "If the woman is a professional, you pay her and that is your sole obligation to her. This way you will know what it is like to have sex and you won't find yourself in a difficult spot." I went on. "Because, you see, I can't tell you what it's like to have sex with a woman. It's something you have to do for yourself."

More food came. Roland instructed me in the proper way to eat the dish. After he was done and before I took the first bite, I turned to him.

"You see, you gave me excellent instructions on how to eat this delicious meal. But before I actually eat it I would know very little about it, would you not agree?"

"I see what you're saying. You want me to taste a woman like I taste this dish?"

"That's it, my friend. That's exactly what I am saying. You see, once in Fiji, while eating a delicious meal, an older woman asked me if I had ever tasted a Fijian woman. If the same question had been asked a hundred years ago, I may have proudly answered that I only ate human flesh from the male warriors I killed in combat. But this was not a hundred years ago, only some months ago. Her younger daughter was sitting nearby and I was afraid she could hear our conversation. I was not sure how to answer the question, so I asked her a question, 'Do Fijian women taste different than other women?'

"Does this meal taste different than meals you have in your country?' she asked back. 'And, don't you like what you eat?'

"I had to answer yes to both her questions.

"So, here in Fiji, we women have a unique taste that you will appreciate only when you try it.'

"I think I blushed, but I had to agree with her wisdom."

Pausing, I looked at Roland and took a sip of my warm beer.

"How much should I pay her?" asked Roland.

"Pay who?"

"The prostitute."

"I don't know. Ask someone who knows. I guess it's like restaurants—you have different prices for different meals."

"I'll find out," concluded Roland.

My stomach was full. Too full to ride a motorbike. I wanted to converse a little more.

"Roland," I remembered to ask, "you know how to protect yourself, right?"

"Protect from what?" he said, looking around for potential threats.

"From sexual diseases!"

"Oh yeah, I watch television, I know about sexual diseases, I know about condoms, how to put it on and how to take it off."

"Always, always protect yourself, Roland. If you don't you'll run into more problems than you can even imagine."

"Don't worry, Régent, I know how to take care of myself."

I was relieved. I wasn't sure if I was talking to an inexperienced teenager, a full-grown man, a wise man or a fool. He is probably all of that, I concluded. Just like I am, like we all are.

After a short walk on the beach, I pulled myself onto the back of his motorbike for the ride back into the city. We followed the ocean for a short time. The warm salty air was the ideal complement to a succulent dinner. I remembered what an old girlfriend had once said to me while riding in my convertible after a delightful meal, which had followed delicious lovemaking.

"You men are always happy when you have sex, food, and a little fun."

I looked at her, acquiescing. "Of course, what else would you need to feel happy?"

She disapproved. "There is more to life than that."

"Right now, at this very moment," I corrected her, "there is nothing more."

But Roland, I thought, never had sex in his entire life.

"How can I miss something I never had?" Roland had answered when I asked him if he misses not having sex. His answer was very realistic and astute. "But if I try sex and can't have it for awhile, I'll probably miss it." After a pause he concluded, "Perhaps it is wiser not to try it."

I couldn't help admiring his common sense while at the same time feeling sad. How can a human being miss out on sex? How can Roland choose to ignore sex? He definitely lives in a different world than mine. To me, Roland was the Other. He was my Other friend. Could his choice be tied to cultural values different than mine? I was puzzled.

The Concept of Culture

Traveling around the world and meeting diverse people brought me to thinking a lot about the much contested and especially elusive concept of culture. Culture is the intellectual concept we refer to when we talk about the differences we find in the Other or when we want to affirm our uniqueness. Travelers are very interested in this topic and know intuitively that any attempt to understand other cultures will immediately present them with the difficulty of understanding and explaining their own culture to others. When I ask Travelers why they are traveling, by far the major reason they voice is to get to know other cultures. But what exactly do we mean by culture?

The semantic field of the word "culture" is not unlike the one for words such as "liberty" or "love." It is expandable and fuzzy. Culture's variables are numerous and divergent depending on how we wish to frame its semantic field. Culture has material, social, spatial, and symbolic dimensions. There are cultural practices and cultural products created by the arts and the media; culture associated with the social indicators of race, gender, class, education, ethnicity, and nation; culture as it takes form within the physical space of neighborhood, city, region, nation, and the world; and culture as a symbolic construct that imparts meaning to our everyday lives. Culture is also a political and ideological tool. These apparently separate dimensions of culture in fact constitute one single ensemble with numerous parts, all in continuous interaction with one another.

But how does a Traveler define culture? To him, cultures are associated with flesh and blood individuals. The basic premise I present here and from which I want to approach this intricate topic is this: culture is to be expe-rienced. Travelers visit places and peoples whose cultures belong to all of us as citizens of the world. Yet, our under-standing of most of those cultures is very modest, often nearly nonexistent. Travelers want to visit other places, meet other peoples, and experience other cultures. They should be commended for trying to enlarge their under-standing of what it is to be human.

All cultures happen at once and all cultures influence one another. We are more aware of this synchronicity of the world cultures today mainly because of the improved communication networks and ease of travel. Travelers are an intrinsic part of today's global mobility. We are more aware of other cultures today than we were only fifty years ago and certainly more aware than we were five hundred years ago. We may also be more aware of our own cultural complexity and the inherent difficulty of defining who we are or understanding the cultural appropriation process that relentlessly molds our identities. Yet, we may fail to recognize the basic human element in all cultures and to remind ourselves that we are human and therefore no stranger to any culture, no matter how foreign it appears to be.

One's culture is deeply ingrained into one's thoughts, feelings, and actions. One's culture is mostly unconscious and difficult to explain to someone else without resorting to clichés or stereotypes. This may be one reason why we tend to generalize and stereotype other cultures, when all we are able to perceive in the Other is the "surface differences" that jumps out at us as not being who we are. The most difficult accomplishment is to look at the differences and focus our attention steadily on what is beyond the obvious. Travelers are constantly reminded that they too are different—they *are* the Other—to the people they meet during their travels.

One cultural issue I struggled with during my travels in India was privacy. It appeared to me that I could never get any privacy in India unless I stayed in my hotel room and locked the door. Even then, privacy never came easy. My Indian friends didn't understand why I wanted to lock myself in my room when I could be with everybody else. They explained to me that I could enjoy my privacy while being with them. They didn't see the need to physically remove myself from their company in order to enjoy my privacy. This concept of privacy wasn't part of my friends' culture. And what my friends suggested was foreign to me.

I was reflecting on this while sitting on a public bench facing the Mississippi River at the Moon Walk in New Orleans. There were many tourists surrounding me but none dared sit on my bench even though it could easily seat two more people. I looked at the other four benches close by to see if they were crowded. One person only was seated on three of the benches and a young couple snuggled on the fourth. Honestly, I was glad nobody came to sit beside me. I enjoyed the privacy of my bench.

There is no such privacy in India. Too many people, too few public benches, yes, but as important as these physical differences are, there is also in India a tangible sense of one's private life being engulfed in the collective public life. I say tangible because it seems to me that this sense of losing yourself in a collective mass has a specific odor, a specific color, a specific sound, and a specific taste that I associate the most with my time spent in India. The odor is pungent as a curry dish, the color blue as young blue Krishna in love with Radha, the sound brass as a marching band, and the taste sweet as condensed milk.

At any rate, this is how it appears to me as one who values the quietness of privacy over the ebullience of the crowds. The latter could be reassuring to some people while being overwhelming to others. I've met Westerners in India who could no longer process the abundance of familiar and novel sounds, odors, and visual stimuli that a walk on a busy Indian street delivers. Many have suffered from acute sensory indigestion. Sometimes they had to regroup behind the closed door of their hotel rooms and some even had to run to the closest airport before the full-blown cultural shock paralyzed them completely.

On the other hand, I have an Indian friend from Calcutta who moved to a large and beautiful house outside Los Angeles after marrying an American woman. They could not visually see their closest neighbor. My friend was astounded by the peacefulness of his environment. At first he prized the calmness of his new life, but after a few months he couldn't bear the stillness anymore. He had grown up with a host of people constantly buzzing around him in a household with no closed doors. He wanted to be physically close to people again even if they were strangers. He pleaded with his wife to move to an apartment in a large building in downtown Los Angeles. She couldn't understand why he wanted to leave such a beautiful house away from the bustle of the city.

Flexibility, compromise, and adaptation are survival tools we constantly use in our daily life, often without realizing that what we are doing is akin to cultural alchemy, extracting gold from the depths of our beings to create our lives.

The ride back home on Roland's motorbike took more time than expected. We ran into heavy traffic downtown, near the newly opened shopping mall. Roland suggested that we stop there for ice cream. I obliged him, but my interest was more in the mall than having ice cream. My stomach was still too full. The crowd inside the mall was unbelievably large and I felt rather queasy among so many people who didn't look like me in a place that looked so much like me, that is, like any other mall in the world. I knew mall culture; but why this uneasy feeling? The mall had only opened the previous day. It was the novel air-conditioned attraction in town and that day the temperature was particularly high.

"Here's some ice cream, Roland," I said, pointing to a small stand behind a long line of people.

"Let's walk around the mall first," he replied.

We walked a very short distance before Roland stopped in front of a store. He knew exactly where he was going.

"Did you come here yesterday?" I asked.

"Yes, there was music for the opening day and a drawing to win a car."

We went in. Roland walked straight to the back of the store and addressed the young salesperson briefly. It seemed to me that everyone working at the mall was less than twenty-five years old. She came back with a vacuum cleaner. Roland looked at it attentively, lifted it up briefly before nodding at the saleswoman. On cue, she dropped an ashtray full of dirt on the immaculate brand new carpet. Roland went to work instantly and cleaned the carpet in no time. I think I saw a half smile on his face, though Roland seldom smiles. He handed back the machine and walked away. I followed him, puzzled. "What was that all about?" I asked him. "Why would you buy a vacuum cleaner? You have no carpet in your house."

His house is a marvel. It was built by the Portuguese in the early seventeenth century and has been in his family for six generations. All the floors are made of concrete and incline slightly toward the back of the house to allow rainwater to wash away to the drain that sits beside by a now-defunct river. The roof has two wide openings to the sky to provide a natural cooling system to the hot and muggy climate of Malacca. My favorite thing to do at Roland's house was to stand under one of the openings and take a rain shower in the middle of the living room during a strong afternoon downpour. Why would he need a vacuum cleaner?

"My family wants to sell the house," Roland explained. "It really belongs to all of us since my parents died some years ago, but I am the only one who wants to live there. That's the only house I've known in my entire life. Besides, all my siblings are married with kids and they prefer modern houses with all the amenities. It costs a lot of money to maintain our family house and I can't afford it anymore if my siblings don't help me with the costs."

He went on. "The vacuum cleaner is for when I move into a modern house. Remember when we went to my sister's house the other day? Remember the vacuum cleaner she showed us? It was just like the one in the store. I think that's the one I want. I never used a vacuum cleaner before today. It's a remarkable piece of equipment, don't you think? I may also buy a dishwasher. Do you have a dishwasher in your house? And a car. I never owned a car before, only a small motorbike. I will probably need a car since my house will not be in the city anymore."

Yes, I did recall a vacuum cleaner being the center of attention in the living room of the brand new house his sister had just bought. I hadn't made much of it at the time, but after what Roland had just told me I began to grasp the compelling significance for him and his siblings of owning a vacuum cleaner. It means a small modern house, wall to wall carpet, washer and dryer, dishwasher, a bathroom with a tub and, of course, a car. The vacuum cleaner was to Roland what the rain shower in the old house was to me: nostalgia for the old in my case and for the new in his. Perhaps we weren't that different after all.

Curious, I asked him, "Are you going to buy the house or the vacuum cleaner first?"

"We have a family meeting next week to decide what to do with the house. If we sell, I will buy the vacuum cleaner before I find my house."

I would have done the same. A week passed before Roland returned home with the vacuum cleaner. I couldn't tell if he was excited and happy or sad.

"The house will be sold?" I asked.

He nodded cheerlessly. I felt sad, very sad. I pictured Roland vacuuming the carpets of his new modern house somewhere in the suburbs of Malacca and missing his beautiful old family house where he was born and had lived all his life. He had to miss it, right? How could it be otherwise? Or was I entirely wrong? Was I projecting my feelings on my friend?

When I came back to Malacca about two months later, Roland was already in his new house. I caught the bus near his old house to go visit him. It took me over an hour to get there. He was waiting in his front yard and greeted me cheerfully. I went in.

"How do you like it?" he asked.

"It's very nice, Roland, very nice."

He sat on his new beige sofa and offered me the matching beige La-Z-Boy recliner. "Would you like a beer?"

"No, thanks. So, how do you like your new life?"

"It's good. I have a car now. It's in the garage. Come see it."

"Great, I'm happy for you. Did you keep the motorbike?"

No, he hadn't. We went to the garage. I wanted to ask about the vacuum cleaner. Roland suggested going for a ride. He had not yet shown me the rest of the house. He never did.

"Let's go eat something," I proposed. We started for the car. "Roland, what about the vacuum cleaner?" I asked as we got in.

"It broke. I have to buy another one."

Arriving at the restaurant, we sat down to eat *nasi minyiak*, rice flavored with cinnamon, cardamom and other spices. When Roland reached for his food, he had the following comment:

"I am very hungry now; I think I'll taste a woman soon."

Bon appétit, Roland. Don't eat too much, and save room for dessert.

One of anthropology's most profound insights is that a person can only express himself within the cultural repertoire that is available and acceptable to that person. Travels widen the availability and deepen the acceptability of cultural behaviors. Seasoned Travelers come to understand that individuals live their lives within the context of many cultures intermingling with one another, overlapping in some areas, or keeping their distance from one another in other areas. The larger framework is the global world. As we become more aware of this global world and the global cultures within it, and of our own cultural specificity, we also become aware of more choices available to us as human beings.

Travelers like to think of culture in terms of a world repertory containing resourceful variations on how to be human. This repertory stretches from the beginning of the human journey to the lives we create for ourselves today, and may even include the ones we imagine living tomorrow. I like this way of thinking about culture because it's creative and exciting. I like to think of culture as the medium of expression for our lives on earth. One's identity is a work in progress.

Advice to Would-Be Travelers

Be yourself, but allow yourself to be the Other, sometimes.

☙ 5 ☙

Transformations

I was riding my motorbike away from the sea, toward
Mount Agung, the highest peak on Bali. Traditional
Balinese houses ideally face the mountains and volca-
noes—not the ocean—where the gods are believed to
reside. I was on my way to greet the gods. It was a Balinese friend, Ketut, who explained to me that the real
beauty and power of the island was found at high altitude.
He did so while we were resting in the shade of a colossal
waringin tree, sacred to the locals and photogenic to the
tourists. Ketut was the reason I undertook this short two
to three day trip to the mountains.

I suppose anyone visiting the stunning island of Bali
can't help but fall in love with it. There is so much to
love in Bali, and its delightful people are the first on the
long list. When I arrived at Denpasar airport early on a
Tuesday afternoon, I felt excited immediately. What I
sensed was that elusive quality we call distinctiveness.
It was in the air we breathed. Bali is in Indonesia, the
fourth most populous country and the largest Muslim
population in the world (approximately eighty-eight per-
cent of Indonesia's total population is Muslim). There are
more than seventeen thousand islands in the Republic of

Indonesia and more than three hundred languages spoken, but Bahasa Indonesia is the official language and is spoken everywhere in Bali.

The Balinese are a Malayan group related to the Javanese. They were converted to Hinduism in the seventh century and Bali later on became a refuge for Hindu Javanese fleeing Islam. Javanese refugees brought with them the gamelans, orchestras of tuned percussion instruments (such as xylophones made of bronze or bamboo, wooden or metal chimes, and gongs) that are still played in Bali. To this day, the Balinese have preserved a highly ritualistic culture that influences every aspect of their lives and includes agriculture, dancing, music, mask carving, folk drama and architecture. This is their life. It is also what attracts so many tourists to Bali. The people of Bali are faced with a constant struggle to achieve equilibrium between their economic prosperity fueled by tourism, and the social cohesion and stability of their population.

Ketut was a flute maker and a mask carver. His family owned rice fields in the countryside of Ubud. Their land had been identified by a group of national and foreign investors based in Jakarta as prime land for a sizeable hotel and recreation center for cultural tourists. The developers who wanted to buy the land at a very good price had already approached Ketut's family. His father categorically refused to sell. Later on Ketut had an idea: Why not use part of the land to build a small hotel for tourists? This way, he argued to his father, we have one foot in each world: the traditional world of agriculture which has sustained the family for many generations and the brave new world of tourism, perhaps the industry of the future for the family.

Ketut was convincing and had his father's ear. The latter asked three questions: How much money do we need to invest to build the hotel? At what interest are we going to borrow it? Who will come to the hotel? Ketut was trying to answer them the best way he could. It is probably how he came to ask me the following straightforward questions:

"Do you like Bali? Are you married?"

He is most likely looking for an associate, I thought. If he finds me a wife, I will stay here and we can run the business together. That is probably what he is thinking at this moment. If I answer yes to the first question and no to the second, my life could be completely transformed at this very moment. A fuzzy vision of a potential blissful married life in Bali flashed across my mind.

"Yes, I love Bali; and no, I am not married," I answered.

That was all he wanted to hear. When I visited him the next day, Ketut was more animated than usual. He told me that his village would be celebrating an important event in three days.

"We would be pleased to have you as our guest."

I thanked him and promised that I would be there. I am a tourist to the Balinese but also a self-proclaimed Traveler. The former is satisfied with the front-stage performance put on by different agents of the Balinese tourism industry while the latter also wants access to the back stage, where the Balinese feel at home and act naturally. While the front stage is well defined and clearly marked, the back stage is more like a vast gray area that only comes into focus intermittently and for brief periods of time. Travelers live for these moments. Unfortunately, they represent rare moments of lucidity that fade away rapidly. My following experience was one such occasion.

I went to Ketut's village on the day of the festivities. He greeted me warmly and introduced me to all his family and friends. When the time came to eat, he seated me across from a beautiful woman who was very young.

"She is my cousin," he said. "Do you think she's pretty?"

That is all he said. I understood what he meant. It was up to me now. I looked at her and smiled. She smiled back. That was the extent of our communication. We never talked. The screen of my mind was blank. The blissful vision was gone. Ketut never mentioned anything else about her. He understood. The day after my visit to the village, I told Ketut that I was heading to the mountains on my motorbike.

"Take this map of the island," he said before bidding farewell.

"I'll see you in a few days, Ketut."

"I'll see you if you come back."

That was the last time we saw each other.

I did not look at Bali's map during my brief trip to Mount Agung. I peeked at it the day after I had left the island. Bali has a convivial shape. It looks like the head of a friendly dog. Travelers love to look at maps because they represent the first stage of transformation. I travel without maps but I like to look at them when I'm not traveling. When I travel I'm living a dream; when I'm at home I dream my life on the road. Maps are mental food that transform realities. Maps represent highly abstract ideas and notions given authority in a very limited space. I am truly fascinated by maps, especially world maps. I can contemplate them for hours, losing myself in intricate details or gently gazing at the overall picture and taking in their beauty. Mentally, they are very stimulating. After studying a beautiful world map, I have a hard time keeping in place. Having contemplated the whole world, how can I keep still?! For a moment, I know the unknown world. It is all there, with different colors for different countries. All the oceans are there, all the mountains. I can see everything.

I get a particular thrill out of maps showing world time zones with the whole world becoming meaningful through time. What an incredible and powerful idea that is! The Greenwich meridian in England becomes the time center of the world and the rest of the world is divided into time zones of 15 degrees longitude each. This schematic was officially adopted in 1884, when, during an international conference, attendees agreed to bestow new meaning to the world through time. England was at the height of its imperial power and the Industrial Revolution was reaching the rest of the world through the development of the steamboat and the railroad. Since 1884, time has become the main measure for productivity.

If you look closely at a world-time-zones map, you will notice how the time zones do not always follow a straight north-south path. On the contrary; and this is the beauty of it, it is all twisted and irregular. There are also a few thirty-minute adjustments here and there. The map I am looking at right now is a Mercator projection that has been used in navigation since the seventeenth century.

Gerardus Mercator (1512–1594) found a way to represent the sphericity of the earth on a flat surface while keeping its shapes intact, even though enlarged. His 1569 world map used the new projection he had recently created and that we still use today. The 1994 Mercator projection I have in front of me as I write these lines gives this cautionary explanation: "It is also the best projection for displaying international time zones. To the north and south distortion increases rapidly as for example South America is actually nine times larger than Greenland."

My very favorite meridian on the map is the 180th meridian. It represents the international date line and separates one day from the next. Flying over the international date line is an exhilarating experience. When traveling across the line in an eastward direction, one moment you are at Sunday noon and the next Saturday noon. Time travel.

Mental Maps

I have a mental map of the world that I carry with me wherever I go. My mental map is a powerful tool for transformation. My travels take place in this world as much as they take place in the real world. Just like the Mercator map, the layout of my world mental map is completely whimsical. On the Mercator map, Europe is on top of the map and the scale of the world projection is more accurate along the equator and its distortion increased dramatically as we move farther away from the equator. Its creator was European. The medieval Ptolemaic-Christian geographers drew their *mappae mundi*, maps of the world, by placing east (Jerusalem) at the top. Their ecumenical maps, aimed at representing the entire inhabited world, showed Jerusalem at the center of the world.

As map scholar Denis Wood (1945–) explained so well in his book *The Power of Maps* (1992), every map has an author, a subject, and a theme. No map is objective, neutral, transparent, or even accurate. My mental map is very personal. There is in it, circumnavigating the equator, a fine thread representing my own rhythm, the beating of my heart. Each country, each parcel of space closer to my rhythm, is a less distorted representation of my being than other countries far away from it. But all pulsate in harmony to the pounding of my heart, only some seem to beat louder.

Those mental spaces, or inner spaces, are populated by billions of beings, speaking millions of languages, and expressing themselves in countless ways. I have met only a minute number of them. Some large stretches of land could be likened to continents separated by vast oceans. I have yet to set foot on many of these continents or to cross most of the oceans. The one major dissimilarity with the Mercator map, however, is that my mental map is continually changing shape and at a rapid pace. Continents are drifting. Countries are uniting while others are breaking away. Old languages die and new ones are created. The only stable part is the thread around the equator. Moreover, I suspect that my inner map has no boundaries. It is infinitely expandable.

Inner space is expandable space. As for outer space, on the one hand it may seem to be finite, it may appear measurable, from one precise point to another. Certainly our physical world appears to be contained within boundaries and, especially in this day and age, it looks as if we know the world's physical dimensions with a precision inconceivable at any previous time in recorded history. On the other hand, the accrued knowledge in quantum physics and molecular biology, the movement of the planets and stars in the night sky and the dance of electrons that is taking place under the scrutiny of the microscope point to an inexhaustible amount of space even in the outer materialized world. It is a question of how we measure space and what our awareness can encompass and comprehend.

Theoretically speaking, there is no limit to the amount of physical space that exists in the universe. Seen this way, outer space is a genuine reflection of inner space, which is not only infinite, but which is also being created and recreated ceaselessly. It is my belief that questions regarding the probable beginning or possible ending of our physical world would be better answered by directing them inwardly, by looking at the creation and passing of our thoughts and feelings. How does a thought begin? And where does it go once created? I see little difference between the birth of a thought and the birth of the universe. And since we create or give birth to thoughts as easily as we breathe, I do not see why it would be otherwise when it comes to the creation of the universe. Poet Rainer Maria Rilke (1875–1926) wrote that there is only one journey, going inside yourself.

We may say that God created the universe. But this statement only begs another question: What is our relation with God? Is not God sharing our inner and outer worlds? Is not God as close to us as our own breath? Is there a difference between God and us? No one can answer these questions for all of us. But each of us can answer them for himself. Each of us knows the precise answer for himself. Maybe the relationship between God and man is the same that exists between inner reality and outer reality. Maybe one is a reflection of the other.

Perhaps God would not mind being thought of as a reflection of man. Perhaps God is generous enough to look into the mirror and see himself/herself/itself in man's reflection. And maybe God is playful enough to turn the mirror back to man, asking, "Who do you see now?" Trappist monk Thomas Merton[10] (1915–1968) wrote something intriguing and enticing about God and man. He said that we find God in our own being, which is the mirror of God. And then he wondered, How do we find our being? He concluded by saying that God's greatest secret is God Himself.

When the Traveler is traveling the outer world, he is also traveling throughout the inner world. It is not important which one he prioritizes. What is important is that he establishes a strong link between the two and that he dedicates himself to deepening it and comprehending the interdependence of the two worlds. The purpose of the journey rests on the strength of that interrelation, which has the power to transform both realities, inner and outer, and thus the very existence of the Traveler. Hence the departure and the return become one motion, and the elegance of the journey resides in the knowing that the farther one goes, the closer he feels to home, not because of the distance traveled, but because he realizes that home has never left him. Once this link is established and it is strong, no difference exists between the inner and the outer worlds, or between the sacred and the profane. Oneness is the reality. Oneness with its infinite expressions. Oneness does not mean sameness.

Returning to my mental map of the world, I can best picture home as the thread encircling the equator of my inner world. It feels true there, at the center of an unlimited universe stretching north and south. Summers and winters coexist simultaneously, as well as dawns and dusks. At any moment, somewhere in my universe, something is possible. In the expandable inner space of

---

10. Thomas Merton, *Thoughts in Solitude* (New York: Dell Publishing Company, 1956).

this universe, everything is always conceivable, always imaginable, and therefore always possible. God, as an intellectual concept, does not exist. That is because, in my inner universe, God permeates every atom of reality. It is there, woven into the fabric of reality, always and perpetually. Therefore, there is no need to intellectually conceptualize His existence or presence. Maybe another English word should be invented to refer to this intent of the sacred I sense in my inner universe. There are some languages spoken today that do not differentiate between the sacred and the profane.

I really like the idea of the equator dividing my inner map into north and south. I like it because it supplies the appositional specifications—or the polarity—of the human condition. If nothing else, each of us comes to know that in any situation reposes the potential for its opposite. At the heart of abundance is the prospect of scarcity. It is in hatred that one comes to recognize love; in war is the desire for peace and in peace the threat of war. It is when one is on the verge of losing something that its value becomes clear. For the Traveler, it is when the decision to come back home is made that the meaning of the journey bursts out into his heart.

I have a theory about special places in the outer world that change the inner landscape of the heart. I call it the Real Estate of the Heart. It is quite simple and is formulated this way: At the center of the world is found one's heart, and locations in the outer world that are attractive to the Traveler shape the inner landscape of the heart, each location increasing in value as it moves closer to the center where the heart itself resides. The Real Estate of the Heart is a thriving enterprise and the value of its real estate is a very private matter that reflects the unique qualities and peculiarities of the individual. Its landscape is exceptionally fluid and malleable. For me, it is my inner map with the equator as my heart radiating north-south. When I travel in the outer world, when I discover new places, meet other people, or when I revisit favorite locations and chat with old acquaintances, I simultaneously rearrange my inner landscape of the heart, reconfiguring the world on my inner map. The Real Estate of the Heart is what brings meaning to travel in the outer world. It is the journey.

The idea of exploring, of discovering or uncovering new segments of reality, outwardly or inwardly, is a commanding impetus for movement. While the age of European exploration beginning in the fifteenth century sought to learn about the outside world, more recently, the explorers of man's emotional and intellectual worlds have wanted to learn about the inside world. But the link between these two realities has always existed. No matter where the point of entry is, from inside or outside, establishing the correspondence between the two transmutes each reality and creates a third one, that of the synthesis. The synergy of outer and inner realities is found in the contradictory aspects of our lives, and its synthesis ushers us toward a new direction, that of a more wholesome understanding of a reality freshly created with each breath we take. Perhaps the fragmentary appearance of our contemporary lives represents an opportunity to assemble disparate aspects of our lives, to examine them closely, one by one and then together, in order to understand who we are and what we do that is us. This us is also each one of us, the unique individual positions at the precise center of the universe, the *axis mundi*, the single individual who knows, beyond any doubt, that life is only possible because of his own unique awareness. Every one of us is invaluable.

The potential for transformation is perhaps the strongest source of motivation for the journey. The genuine transformation offers the Traveler an occasion to be more of who he already is. It is not just a truism to say that to learn about the world is to learn about ourselves. What the world is and represents and who we are and represent as human beings complement each other. Together we are one. Together we stand for the full potential of life on earth. Together we give shape and value to infinite expressions of life forms. Together we create reality and give various names to its many manifestations. Apart, we marvel at the Other's capacity for transformation and how profoundly it impresses us. Apart, we purposely forget that the togetherness of our apparent separate realities is the very substance of the journey. Apart, we also forget that both of us are on this journey together.

Thus, to travel the world is an immense joy. To taste its prodigious diversity is a privilege that yields tremendous pleasure and excitement. One should always be grateful for this opportunity. However, the diversity encountered in the outer world would not be recognized if it were not also present in each of us. The world with its mountains, valleys, rivers and oceans would not exist without their equivalences in us. The world outside resonates to the world inside and vice versa. The diversity in one human being is at least as great as the diversity found in the world outside.

How could it be otherwise? Other peoples, other places, and other times are all present in the heart of every single human being. One person represents unlimited diversity. It is all there inside, ready to be recognized outside and brought back home in the human heart. To honor the diversity inside our hearts is to develop a vision of who we sense we are while recognizing, incarnating, and manifesting its expressions in the world.

Nook was the prettiest Mafioso I had ever met. Not that I knew many members of the Mafioso. Nook, though, a woman in her late thirties from the lower southern gulf province of Phatthalung in Thailand, was rather attractive and friendly . . . and a self-proclaimed Mafioso. Her English was limited but consistent. Her stories were unlimited but inconsistent. She had been married to an American once.

"Husband no good to me," she said. "Have to get rid of husband." She had visited New York ("a nice place"), San Francisco ("pretty but too many hills"), and Chicago ("too many tall buildings . . . give me pain in neck").

"I don't want men anymore," she had told me when we met. "Perhaps better I like women now." She laughed.

Nook was great company. She was always ready to laugh and had entertaining stories to tell. The problem was that most of her listeners only half believed them. She also liked to drink Mekong rice whiskey and she drank it like a man. It was while intoxicated that she told us how she ended up spending two years in jail for a crime she committed in her native town of Phatthalung.

"Me, my family, big Mafia in Phatthalung," she began the story. She went on describing the customary activities of a Mafioso family business such as gambling, protection, arms selling, and fantastic real estate acquisitions. "But no prostitution, no drugs," she insisted. "My family never involved in prostitution or drugs."

Nook made a lot of money. Too much money, according to her assessment. "Too easy, too easy; money comes too easy and too fast."

She lived the life of a movie star, treated her friends to expensive restaurants and lavish gifts. Because she always paid for her expenses with cash, she had to carry a lot of it on her. And because of the cash, she hired a bodyguard. She also never left home without her handgun. One evening, after a good meal and lots of Mekong whiskey, she asked her bodyguard, who was also her driver, to take her home. She never made it home.

As soon as she stepped out of the restaurant she was ambushed and kidnapped by four men dressed in black wearing ski masks. Her bodyguard was knocked down unconscious, but Nook suspected that he was involved in the operation. She was kept in a small dark room for three days. They treated her well.

"They give me good food and plenty of whiskey. I know the money will come so I don't worry too much. My only thinking is to find my bodyguard and beat him up."

After her family paid the money, Nook was free to leave. She went straight to work finding out who had kidnapped her, and after her suspicions about her bodyguard (who had mysteriously disappeared) were confirmed by one of her kidnappers, who confessed that the bodyguard was behind the ambush, Nook tracked him down. He was still living in Phatthalung and not too far from her house.

"He's so stupid. Should be far away, not my neighbor."

"He tells me what happens. I respect him for that. For him, it's business, no problem. But he's my bodyguard, I pay him to work for me. No good. Very bad. I go to his house with my brother and his friend. I tell him that I have no more respect for him. He cries. Think I am going to kill him."

Nook fired twice, one bullet in each knee. She crippled him. Her brother's friend turned her in to the police. She did two years. Thus was Nook's story as told by Nook.

"Now, I'm a different woman," Nook insisted. "I drink little. No smoking. Have no gun. Little money. I live simple life. I travel. Meet people. I no big Mafia now!"

I didn't know what to believe from her story, but it was a great story. She was certainly not your average Thai woman, and one could tell, by observing her daily behavior and interaction with others, that she had a brawny presence that commanded respect from others, men or women. How did she get rid of her husband, I thought to myself. Better not to ask.

I had known Nook for about ten days when I decided it was time for me to leave. I had already explained to her how Travelers never stay in one place for too long.

"Better this way," she had told me. "Better not to become too attached to people you meet. I feel same. Where you going?"

I hadn't yet decided where I was going, but I told her I was heading south toward the Malaysian border.

"Go visit my family in Phatthalung," she suggested. "I call them today. Call my sister. She has big house. I tell her you come soon."

How could one say no to Nook? I couldn't. Besides, I really had nowhere to go. Here was a wonderful occasion to visit a region few tourists or Travelers know. Phatthalung was once known as a hotbed for Thai communist insurgents and legend had it that kids learn how to shoot a gun before they can walk. Today, it is better known for its large fishing and prawn farms.

"My sister runs a prawn farm there," said Nook. "It's family business."

"What about the Mafioso business?" I asked. "Is your sister a Mafioso?"

She laughed out loud. "No, no, my sister never Mafioso. She can't shoot. Her husband can't shoot. Can only catch prawns."

It took me a long time to arrive in Phatthalung. I had to change buses three times and wait between rides. When I finally made it to the bus station in the small town where Nook's sister lives, just outside Phatthalung, I looked on the map Nook had drawn for me to see how to reach the house. What a beautiful map it was! It was a perfect map of how to get lost and eventually find your way by asking someone where to go. It was so much like my friend Nook.

I started to walk and was soon completely lost. The map worked. I was also hungry and decided to get something to eat. After the meal, I opted to try one more time to find my way to Nook's sister's and, if that failed, I'd call. I finally located a bank on the map and made the left turn indicated. I was prompted to walk about one kilometer until I saw a four-way junction. I did as instructed, but the one kilometer turned out to be more like three kilometers.

I turned right at the junction and walked another half hour before I spotted a large house with two smaller houses nearby. It fit Nook's description. I went to the main house and knocked at the door. Nobody answered. When I turned around to go to one of the smaller houses, Lek was standing right in front of me.

"Hi, my name is Lek," she said in excellent English. "You are Nook's friend?"

"Yes, my name is Régent. I am from Canada. And you speak English so well and you are so young!"

"I am not young. I am twelve. I want to learn more English with you," said Lek. "My mother is coming soon. Are you hungry?"

I was not hungry but I said I was. Lek was pleased. She knew exactly what to do. She sat me down at the dining table in the smaller house to the left of the main house and served me a savory meal of red curried fish and prawns. During the meal, Lek told me that she was studying English at school and that she had a pen pal in England. She also wanted to go to England one day to meet her friend and to study there.

"Where do you live?" she asked.

"I live in New Orleans, in Louisiana, in the United States."

"Why you don't live in your country, in Canada?"

"It's too cold in Canada. And I am like you, I like to travel and live in different places."

"Maybe one day, I go live with you in New Orleans," said Lek.

I took a nap. When I woke up, Lek was ready to take me to meet her family. None of them spoke English. Lek was the translator. I met her mom, dad, half sister, and brother. I also met a friend of the family, a young rather gloomy girl. She paid no attention to me. Later on, Lek told me that she had just returned from a month-long trip to have an abortion. According to Lek, the girl's boyfriend, an older married man, paid for everything but did not want to have anything to do with her anymore.

"But Lek," I said, "you are so young, how come you know all those things?"

"I am twelve! I am not young! Can I sleep with you tonight?" she asked.

"Well, ask your mother first."

She ran away and came back a few minutes later. "She said yes."

It was a very large bed divided in three by two long and narrow pillows. I slept in the first slot to the left, Lek slept in the middle slot . . . and the young gloomy girl who had just had an abortion paid for by her ex-boyfriend, the older married man, slept in the last slot on the right. I didn't realize she had slept with Lek and me until morning. She had come to bed very late and complained of a splitting headache when she woke up, also late. Lek told me that the gloomy girl was looking for another boyfriend.

The long narrow pillows on Thai beds are like thin walls separating rooms in Western houses. They are powerful symbolic divisions and one does not cross them lightly. I first wondered how the family could let me sleep in the same bed with the young gloomy girl. Then I came to the understanding that the long narrow pillows and young Lek in between us acted as a strong deterrent against any illicit business between us. It was not that I felt attracted to her, but in my culture a man and a woman do not sleep in the same bed unless they are already intimate, or desire to be intimate. with one another. Apparently not here, at least not in this family.

Nook's family treated me extremely well. I called Nook to thank her. The morning I left, I met other members of Nook's family, the Mafioso family. Yes, they were carrying guns, and yes they had bodyguards. None spoke

English. Once more young Lek was a brilliant interpreter. They were awfully nice to me. Everybody came to the bus station, even the gloomy girl. Lek was crying and made me promise that one day she could come to New Orleans to live with me and study English. I promised. The gloomy girl was the first one back in the car. Lek was the last one to wave me off. She had a message from the gloomy girl.

"She wants you to know she likes sleeping with you."

I was on my way to Malaysia. I had no maps.

On my mental map I often visualize four large continents. I am quite active on these continents. On each continent there is one city or a region that I know well and where I often go to work, relax, or simply visit because I am interested in what is going on there. These cities or regions correspond to cities or regions that I have also come to know during the course of my life. One is the city of Sherbrooke in Québec where I was born. Another is New Orleans where I have lived most of the last twenty-two years and includes the nearby towns of Pensacola and Destin on the Gulf of Mexico in Florida.

Another region is in Mexico where I have studied, taught, and frequently worked (and still do). It includes the cities of San Miguel de Allende and Guanajuato in the center of the country, the capital, Mexico City, as well as the beautiful Pacific coastal towns of San Patricio-Melaque, Barra de Navidad and Puerto Vallarta.

Finally, a fourth region is in Southeast Asia. While I may picture the southern islands of Thailand or other islands off the east coast of Malaysia when thinking about this region, oddly it also includes the city of Kathmandu, Nepal, and its valley. I will explain why momentarily.

These four regions and cities that I know and love can be visited by anyone who decides to do so and who has the means to travel there. Actually, some of them are among the most visited tourist destinations in the world. So why would they be so special to me? Specific mental and affective dispositions are associated with these locations. Sherbrooke, of course, is where I grew up. It is family, a sense of security and affection but also of limitation since I spent only my childhood and teenage years there, though none of my adult years. I left for good when I was nineteen. Therefore, others often made many decisions affecting my life while I lived in Sherbrooke. New Orleans is the city where I've spent many of my adult years up to now. It is a city I have chosen to live in and of which I am very fond. New Orleans is home. It is where I am the most comfortable right now and where my life seems to flow most naturally. It is like slipping into an old, worn-out sandal. The fit is perfect precisely because the sandal is anything but perfect.

Pensacola and Destin I visited for the first time a few weeks after I arrived in New Orleans. I remember reading about Destin in 1983 in a travel brochure I found on the plane on my way to New Orleans. A photograph of crystal-clear emerald waters and sugar-powder white sand beaches caught my attention. I also remember being surprised to learn that the place itself was actually prettier than the picture. Pensacola and Destin have since been my favorite retreats from city life and places where I often go to make important decisions in my life. I have always associated the rhythm of the ocean waves with the beating of my heart. It has always seemed so much easier to make a decision when the beating of my heart is amplified by the rhythm of the ocean. It still does. Destin and Pensacola have always been places of transformation, places where I learn to know more about who I am.

Mexico represents a comfortable place to be, but never sufficiently comfortable to completely relax. In other words, Mexico has always been a place where a lot of learning takes place. For one thing, I speak Spanish well enough to interact with Mexicans but not well enough to fully integrate their lifestyle. This basic and moderate use of the language that I command is often misleading because while I may comprehend the literal meaning of the words I hear or pronounce, the sociocultural content these words possess may not get across my understanding clearly. Distortions, both minor and major, occur. Nonetheless, so many traits of the social life of Mexicans appeal to me that I feel quite at home there.

I love to take my afternoon meal around 3 P.M. and a light late snack before going to bed. I don't mind getting a late start at work in the morning and working later during the evening. Every time I am back at home in the United States, I miss terribly walking the Zócalo, the central public space found in all towns and cities in Mexico, small or large. Here, infants, kids, teenagers, their parents, grandparents, and great-grandparents congregate in the early evening. Music, social chat, flirting, eating, or accepting flowers from a secret admirer are the main activities carried on in this central public space. How I miss this back home. I believe there is no better place for children to grow up than Mexico and definitely no better place to be in the whole world on Sundays in the late afternoon and early evening.

The region I have labeled Southeast Asia is the most foreign to me, thus the most fascinating and enticing. For one thing, I do not speak any of the languages spoken there. The conversations I have there take place in Basic English, the recent *lingua franca* of planet earth. It has been learned by many, not just as a second language but often as a third or fourth language. Some 1.5 billion people worldwide speak English in varying degrees of proficiency.

In this region of the world, I cannot read any written signs, newspapers, or menus at the restaurants unless they are also translated into Basic English. It is in this region of the world, more than anywhere else, that I feel things rather than comprehend them with my rational mind. When there, my capacity for feeling things in order to understand what is going on is far greater than when I am elsewhere. Because of my strong desire to relate to situations I encounter there and to connect to the people involved in those situations, over time I have developed a skill for feeling things out. The skill I refer to, one that became a part of me while I was traveling in Southeast Asia, is actually the natural way we communicate with each other. Communication in words, using intellectual concepts, is only one manifestation of this underlying heart-to-heart ability to communicate that we all possess, irrespective of one's culture or the language spoken.

In Thailand, for instance, where the majority of inhabitants are Buddhist, there is a solicitude toward other persons that prompts a stranger to sit next to you if you happen to be sitting alone. The thoughtful stranger does not have to utter a word to you. He comes simply to share his presence because you were alone. Nobody should be alone in the world, the stranger is gently saying, and we all have the same need for companionship. Often, words only mask this vulnerability we sense within ourselves and in others. In our fast-paced societies we have fewer opportunities to share each other's presence in silence without feeling uncomfortable or unproductive. What are we afraid of?

The continent or region of my inner map that corresponds to the region I have labeled Southeast Asia on the world map is one of clarity and mystery. It has clarity because there I can let go of the artifices of social conventions such as language and perceive reality with my heart. It has mystery because when there I sense the full potential of what is imaginable, yet still to be fully manifested. Both inwardly and outwardly, this region of Southeast Asia is, in the best sense of the word, an enigma. And I welcome the enigma, as I respect and enjoy its bounty.

I include in this region of clarity and mystery I call Southeast Asia one particular city and its surrounding valley: Kathmandu. I didn't spend a lot of physical time in the valley of Kathmandu. While in the city I met and hired a young Nepalese man, probably in his mid-thirties, to be my guide for a week or so as we walked from village to village throughout the valley. I initially hired him for two reasons: First, he claimed to speak English and second, I liked him. It turned out that even though he definitely spoke a highly personal version of English—which came in handy for communicating very basic information such as when or where to eat, when to stop, and where to sleep—his use of it was so eccentric that I seemed to understand him better when he spoke his native language than when he spoke English. I never told him this because I didn't want to depreciate his achievement.

Instead I told him, in Basic English, some of which he seemed to understand, that I wanted to learn Nepalese and would love to hear him speak in his native tongue.

When he did, I of course couldn't understand a word of it. He said nothing about me not understanding anything he said, probably because he didn't want to offend me. Then, after a few days, something wonderful happened. Not being able to understand each other's language, we fell silent for long periods of time as we walked side by side. It was then that I came to realize that I could understand my friend much better when we were not talking to each other but were sharing each other's presence.

I liked my friend and when I was aware of his presence and offered mine in return we seemed to understand each other very well. I trusted him as my guide. I followed him wherever he wanted to take me. I met many of his family members living in different villages in the valley. I took meals with them, slept by their side and offered my company in exchange for their company. I had the best time in the Kathmandu Valley. I will never forget my friend, who insisted on being called Nelson, and our long silent communications while walking in the beautiful valley of Kathmandu. I hope that he feels the same way. To this day, I still do not know what name he gave me.

There is one huge sprawling city in Mexico, one of the most populated cities on earth right now, with well over twenty million inhabitants living within its confines. This modern city rose from the ruins of a precolonial island city, Tenochtitlán, which served as the capital city of the Aztec Empire until 1521. When the Spanish took over, under the leadership of explorer Hernán Cortés, they tore down the pyramids in the central city and built a cathedral on the same site that is still standing today, even though it is leaning due to frequent earthquakes. The Spaniards renamed it Mexico City.

On my inner map, Mexico City is a place of tremendous motion and of great hope because, there, the past and the future have nowhere to point to except the present. This is because in Mexico City the present is constantly reinterpreted through its past, a past very visible in the architecture and layout of the city and on the physiognomies of its inhabitants. The city is also understood in relation to its hope for a better future, which can be deciphered on every face seen on its streets. Mexico City is a place of great transformation because the present city encompasses all the probable pasts and probable futures. It is all there for anyone to see. Mexico City is adamant about living only in the present.

Before Mexico City began to look like the overgrown and out-of-control sprawl that it is today, it was a rather ordered and peaceful metropolis organized around neighborhoods, many still functioning today in the older parts of town as small distinct communities. In fact, most visiting Mexico City for the first time are astounded to notice the spirit of community still intact in the old town and the feel of a normal city they experience while walking its streets. This may be due to the paucity of high-rise buildings in the downtown area that many people associate with large cities. Mexico City instead sprawls horizontally and, as most visitors stay in one small area—the historic district—it does not have the allure of a gigantic metropolis.

Mexico City has a subway that is inexpensive and efficient. It is accessible to all and is used by some five million people a day. I like Mexico City and, to me, riding its subway to go somewhere I have never been is always a rewarding experience. What I like to do is randomly choose a station as my destination, take the subway there, walk around the neighborhood, have coffee or eat there and later on figure out a way to go back to my hotel on foot. This may take the whole day. It never ceases to amaze me that I can find within one city an infinite range of urban environments to get acquainted with. Each time I go back to Mexico City I go back to a different city. Of course this should be the case for any destination, but it's never as noticeable to me as it is in Mexico City. It is my city par excellence for transformation, probably because the intent of the city is to be firmly grounded in the imperative present.

I am also very fond of the twin small beach resort towns of San Patricio-Melaque and Barra de Navidad found about midway on the Pacific Coast of Mexico. I first went there to conduct field research for my dissertation. I arrived at the small bus station of Melaque at dawn on a weekday after an overnight first-class bus ride from Guadalajara. The serpentine ride through the Sierra Madre mountains left a good half dozen passengers feeling sick to their stomachs and the rest of us very nauseated and breathing through our mouths. I was with my travel companion of the day, a rock-climber from Québec I had met in the youth hostel in Guadalajara. As we finally climbed off the bus, grateful beyond reason to breathe fresh air, we started walking toward the beach nearby. We sighted the ocean as the sun was rising. I loved Melaque at first sight.

I was also in Melaque to celebrate the weeklong festivities in honor of Saint Patrick, the local patron saint. Festivities for a town's patron saint are taken very seriously in Mexico, with fireworks every night in the Zócalo, bull races, a *feria* complete with amusement rides, *ranchera* music blasting from every corner of the Zócalo and an abundance of festivity foods to be sampled. There is a feeling of easiness and childlike enjoyment pervading the air during the whole week and, if one knows how to avoid confrontation when too much alcohol turns the local men into incensed out-of-control machos, the whole experience is never to be forgotten. I had the best of times that week.

But what really makes this location so endeared to me is the gorgeous two-kilometer beach walk along the Bahía de Navidad between the two towns of Melaque and Barra. At the beginning of the beach strip in Melaque, the ocean is usually subdued, perfect for swimming, and I can look at the beautiful houses built along the beach. As I leave the town, the houses become fewer and the ocean waves a bit more imposing. A sensation, initially almost imperceptible, of leaving a somewhere to enter a nowhere slowly infiltrates my consciousness.

Then, and almost magically, I look around and find myself standing in between a beautiful and peaceful lagoon on my left, with palm trees, egrets, and other marine birds visible in the foreground of the soaring mountains of the Sierra Madre in the distance, and on my right the stunning and staggering Pacific Ocean with waves reaching higher than the mountains, or so it seems. The transition that began so innocently and unnoticeably only an instant before is now complete. I've entered a new territory and at once I recognize its grounds. It is the territory of the nowhere.

This territory is a state of transition, a connecting parcel of land between two destinations or a connecting psychological link between two states of consciousness, two states of awareness. Again, to use another of my favorite English words, it is a place of transformation. To me, this nowhere is an entrancing and intriguing place.

I walked this narrow stretch of sandbar nearly every day during my first month-long stay there and each time it had the same effect on me. Each time I found myself suspended between two worlds, that of the lagoon and that of the sea; between two destinations, Melaque and Barra; between two realities, that of the inner world and that of the outer world. Walking the grounds of nowhere, I found myself somewhere, between Melaque and Barra, somewhere where I could be absolutely anywhere. Little physical movement was ever required. Only awareness. Awareness of infinite possibilities. There, in the stillness of the nowhere, I found the everywhere.

Sometimes my mind was racing so fast I felt dizzy. At other times there was only the awareness of the stillness of my mind. Sometimes, between Melaque and Barra, my hand reached for the notebook in my small pack only to find the blueprint of my inspiration fading quickly, as if it were cheap ink washed away by water. At other times, there was not enough ink in my pen to attempt to translate the deeply stirred emotions I felt throughout my body. Walking, walking nowhere, I believe that my body is a deep receptacle that could contain all of the magnificence and all the knowledge of the nowhere, and that somehow, at some point, I will be able to find an appropriate way to express what I experience in the moment. But when should I stop walking—receiving—and start writing—expressing? I do not know. All I can do is try time after time to reach this delicate balance.

A little farther north of San Patricio-Melaque, facing the gorgeous Bahía de Banderas, is the very well known coastal town of Puerto Vallarta. I first paid a visit to PV (as it is known by many vacationers) when I was in Melaque, with the intention of staying a couple of days, thinking I would not really like it. I stayed one month. The old town of Vallarta won me over, as did the ravishing beaches farther south such as Playa Conchas Chinas, Playa Estacas, Playa Gemelas, Playa Las Animas, and Playa Yelapa. What I like to do best in Vallarta is catch a morning bus somewhere south, say Mismaloya, and take the rest of the day to come back downtown combining beach walking with riding a bus whenever walking on the beach is not possible. In the evening I like to walk the length of the *Malecón* (a wide seaside walkway) that stretches for about ten blocks, get some hot water for my green tea from the local MacDonald's and sit on a bench to watch people pass by while listening to *son* music pouring out of the Cuban club.

A little later on I walk back to my hotel in the heart of old Vallarta, taking a slight detour to pass by the shingle beach to hear the rumble produced by the ebb of the tide shifting the pebbles. I find this singular low-pitched sound intoxicating and evocative. After listening to it for a few minutes I feel lightheaded and have to leave. However, some nights, the sound returns in my dreams; it fills the entire room with balcony that I rent at Hotel Villa del Mar at the corner of Madero and Jacarandas, some six blocks from the ocean front. On these nights the sound wakes me up. I can still hear it for a couple of seconds while my eyes are wide open. Then it exits through the open windows, washes the balcony clean, goes down onto Jacarandas to the Río Cuale and back to the shingle beach from where it emanated. Suddenly I find myself a pebble in the ocean. The realization is swift: I am the rumble. I am that sound. It is the sound of perpetual motion and it is who I am. I am perpetual motion.

Puerto Vallarta is a place I often visit in my inner world. On my mental map, it is very close to the equator where distortions about my true identity are the smallest. It feels remarkably free there, airy, with earth and sea colors particularly buoyant and appealing. When I visit this place, I always picture myself walking at a moderately paced stroll along the immense Pacific Ocean. Every so often I stop to breathe in the salty air, let my vision rest on the horizon, at this visual borderline where it is impossible to distinguish the sea from the sky, and to feel my skin and bones absorbing the warmth of the sunrays. I walk naked. At night I wear ample light cotton clothes in pastel colors with loose leather sandals to walk the *Malecón*. I am often there whenever I feel depressed. Oddly, I never swim in inner Vallarta. I prefer to go somewhere else to swim.

There are places in the outer world that live a full and independent life in my inner world. Vallarta is one such place, as are Pensacola and Destin in Florida, the Kathmandu Valley in Nepal or a certain hidden cove on an island off the east coast of Malaysia that I visited once and for merely a couple of hours. This cove is accessible only by sea and I swam for one hour to get there. Komodo dragons inhabit the small beach. I had never seen them in their natural environment before and they left an indelible impression on me. They own the beach and I felt that whatever I wanted to do there, I had to have their permission first. I observed them from the water for most of the time until I noticed a large flat rock at the right corner of the beach a respectable distance from them. I knew that I could stay there without threatening their sovereignty over the beach. I frequently dream of this cove, its swaggering Komodo dragons lazing in the sun and the sensuousness of crystal-clear waters enshrouding my entire body.

A Traveler is always traveling with his inner compass. My inner compass points to the magnetic equator where my heart resides. A Traveler is always carrying his inner map of the world, and the locations he visits in the outer world alter the configuration of his inner map. Travels in time and space impact the whole being of the Traveler, who himself also exists beyond time and space. Locations in the outer world take on a whole new dimension in the inner world, beyond time and space, and in turn they also affect how Travelers perceive the world in time and space. Places do not exist independently of how we perceive them. We constantly translate the nature of their existence and the heart does the translation. The two worlds are interconnected; as long as we are Travelers, one cannot exist without the other. Once more, the purpose of the journey is to become aware of this interchange between what the eyes see and what the heart feels. The journey probably ends when the heart and the eyes see and feel the same. Then, a new journey is likely to begin.

Terra Australis Incognita: Creativity and Authenticity

When I typed the first line for this book, I had already begun putting restrictions on my creativity. With each subsequent line came more limitations. That was the price I paid to express myself this way. However, the entire time I wrote this book, I knew that I could come back and change anything I wanted. I could erase any sentence I wanted. I could even delete everything and start all over again, this time from a completely different perspective, or write about an entirely different topic. I did all of the above before the conclusion of this book. But only the blank screen on my computer provides me with infinite possibilities, with unlimited creativity. The typing of the first word brings limitations. But it also offers opportunities for transformation.

This is also how I feel about myself, R. J. Cabana, born in Sherbrooke, now living in New Orleans with his wife, Sandra, and German shepherd, Laola, who loves to travel and is currently writing a book about the sheer joy of traveling light. Each of those attributes that describe me also confines my identity as a person who feels most comfortable when nothing is said and everything is conceivable. The nature of our existence is more like a blank screen at this profoundly creative moment before any word is chosen to be written down and all possibilities may still be considered.

Every single person represents to everyone else an immense *Terra Australis Incognita* on their inner map of the world, the imagined unknown southern land on the world map of the Greco-Roman-Egyptian astronomer and geographer Ptolemy (c. 90–c. 168). Whenever I have met someone living a life very different than mine, I have often thought that I could be this person at some creative point in my existence. But above all, I know deep inside my being that before something definitive could be said about anything, all is possible and my creativity recognizes no limits, sees no boundaries. Thus this *I*, who sustains my existence as R. J. Cabana, could be anybody or anything. The curiosity of this being, its sense of experimentation, is unquenchable. When I go to sleep at night in my house in New Orleans, I often dream of those counterpart lives I lead on *Terra Australis Incognita*.

Travelers dream of authentic experiences through the Other. How are we to define authenticity? Is one society more authentic than another? Maybe the tourist is looking for authenticity in the outer world. Maybe he sadly feels that this all-important quality is missing in his own life. And maybe he'll experience glimpses of what was once part of his real or imagined everyday life. Maybe he'll even be able to bring some of this elusive quality back home. Or perhaps some shrewd and clever entrepreneur will find a way to bottle authenticity and sell it to the tourist. Even so, the tourist may then question the authenticity of the bottle of authenticity. And the quest will go on forever. While tourists are consumers of authenticity, Travelers are experimenters of authenticity. At best, they measure authenticity against their inner map of the world. The closer they bring the experience, any experience, near the equator on their inner map, the more authentic it is. Authenticity, therefore, is entirely dependent on one's creativity. Moreover, each individual person is the sole judge of authenticity.

There is no authenticity save that of one's own beating heart. Authenticity emanates from that heart. It is the source of all that exists—us, gods and God included. Our task is to get in touch with the rhythm of our beating heart and to believe that its thrust can lead us home. How can we deny the legitimacy of our own beating heart? It is what keeps us alive, beyond life and beyond death. It is the pulse of life, all life. It is the source of all authenticity.

To Be Human

To be human is to accept transformation. One of my favorite anthropologists, Dorothy Lee[11] (1905–1975), writes about the "larger community of humanness." I like her choice of words to describe the connectivity and complementarity of all social and cultural groups of humans, and ultimately of all individuals. Although too often overlooked, each of us, before anything else, is a human being and an integral part of the larger community of humanness. Without this basic comprehension we will never begin to fathom our differences and cherish them for being unique and exciting expressions of what it means to be human. This larger community of humanness signifies two things: We are all the same; and each of us is unique and invaluable. We are each the same in our humanness, yet fiercely unique in our spirit.

Within the larger community of humanness are seven billion individuals currently making their home on planet Earth and each one is contributing to the variety of the human experience. How many human beings have been born and have died on earth since the beginning of our human story? Who can venture an educated guess? How much knowledge have we amassed since? How can we measure and, most importantly, evaluate knowledge?

The world population is projected to reach nine billion by the year 2050. Each of us is, in a way, stretching the limits of the human condition. Travelers are like scouts eager to sample the diversity of humanness. I consider curiosity to be, and hope it truly is, a fundamental human attribute. What is it to be human? What can we hope for as human beings? We are constantly hoping. Hoping for

11 Dorothy Lee, *Valuing the Self: What We Can Learn from Other Cultures* (Upper Saddle River, NJ: Prentice-Hall, 1976).

a better job. Hoping for a better relationship with loved ones. Hoping for better health. Hoping for a better world. Sometimes we are hoping to die, a legitimate desire that is sadly often denied in many of our societies. Hope is the elusive beauty of life. When it is present, our lives are preciously unrestricted and attractive.

We are perpetually curious. We know about intellectual curiosity, a burning hunger for knowledge. Intellectual curiosity is highly praised in this day and age. But we are also, perhaps to an even greater degree, emotionally curious. We want to know how it feels to be in all kinds of life situations. We yearn to experience life's myriad possibilities. Actually, it is more than emotional curiosity. It is a longing to experience being in different settings. I will call it "being curiosity."

The question really is "What is universal to all human cultures?" What are the basic traits of all human beings? We are born, we die. We need food and shelter. We live together. We seek emotional and mental nourishment. We want to be respected for who we are. We love to laugh. What are the basic traits, really?

In her extensive fieldwork as an anthropologist, Dorothy Lee was often puzzled by what she called the "exorbitant behaviors" she found in other cultures. She found that those extremes of human behavior did not make sense to a reasonable mind, even to an anthropologist accustomed to observing and explaining a wide range of human behaviors. The only conclusion she could reach was that these behaviors were inexplicable to her own mind, even to her broad mind, that they could not be framed inside the Western concept of motivation. Rather, these behaviors represented some other kind of "autonomous motivation" that is very hard for an outsider to understand. Her insight that each culture contains its own definition of what it is to be fully human is relevant to the Traveler, who desires more than anything else to gain a holistic understanding of what it means to be a human being, a member of this larger community of humanness.

The disposition of the Traveler is that of someone forever curious about the next location and the next stranger. At the same time, the Traveler is always hopeful. He never stops hoping that the next destination he visits will be his paradise on earth. To me, the Traveler is the quintessential human being and his journey in the world our journey on earth. The personage of the Traveler is an eloquent metaphor for human inquisitiveness and human aspiration.

The fundamental attribute of the journey is its transformative power, its proficiency at mutating the very being of the Traveler. I have yet to meet a Traveler who does not long to be regenerated by the process of journeying. I have also never met anyone who does not wish to change at least one thing about himself or his life situation. Why is this? Why do we ceaselessly seek change, yet fear it? The nature of change lies in movement. When something changes, when we change, we move from one point to another. We accept new beliefs about reality, both objectively and subjectively. We reject old beliefs about that same reality. Fear is always a part of any change. Change is present in the entire natural world, but to fear change is naturally human. To feel fear is also naturally human. Fear permeates the very fiber of humanness. There is always a reason to fear something, anything. The human thought process is creative because it amalgamates fear with hope of fearlessness. Fear is relentless and circular.

To hope is also part of the genetic backbone of humanness. At least, or at last, one may come to know that if there is meaning to life on earth, and I believe there is, it must reside in the fundamental emotions of human life that include feeling depressed, insecure, doubtful, lost, yet also hopeful, invariably hopeful. The meaning of life is a mystery and will always remain a mystery. In my opinion, an accurate assessment of being human was given by Bernard Loomer (1912–1985), once dean of the Divinity School at the University of Chicago, who is reported to have said the following: "We are born in mystery, we live in mystery, and we die in mystery." It is a mystery we always hope to solve. Sometimes we feel depressed when we fail to understand life. To know life is to know it is a stirring mystery, that of our existence and the stunning vitality and resilience of our lives on earth. This mystery is not dead. The mystery is alive. It is not declared dead and done with. It is alive and transforming itself every day of our lives. This may be why we began this human journey in the first place. It may be why we do not give up when our human lives become unbearable. We want to stay alive in order to have more opportunities to deepen our understanding of the mystery. The mystery becomes an opening, a deep well from which we draw inspiration to live our lives.

Have you ever noticed that the closer you are to someone, the more mysterious this person becomes? The closer you get to the mystery of the person, the more alive and elusive he becomes. The same is true for oneself. We become a mystery to ourselves the moment we touch the core of our being. Then the mystery turns into an opening, an invitation to step into a cool and breezy night after a hot and scorching day. The night stretches eternally as we walk comfortably by the ocean, at home in the mystery of life itself.

The Traveler is curious about the world he visits and he always hopes that the best is yet to come, that the next location, the next encounter will enlighten the purpose of the journey in a way previously unknown. Often, though, he fails to understand the meaning of the journey. He feels depressed. He hits a wall. He hits rocks bottom. Ironically, it is only when he gives in to the overwhelmingly depressing emotions he feels, when he accepts them for what they are, a part of the human journey, only then will he move through them to clarity. The lucidity gained from this experience brings a sobering understanding: the process of the journey is what matters. The enlightening journey commands an elegance that is quite humbling to the intellect: What matters is now, not yesterday, not tomorrow, but right here right now.

Legacy: The *Anima Mundi*

The cultural ethos of Western modern living calls for us to be seekers, explorers, adventurers, travelers and conquerors: all agents of transformation. Jungian psychologist Robert Johnson[12] (1921–) writes about how we have to search to realize that there is no search. He illustrates this Western attribute of our psyche with the Chinese story of the fish that grandly announces its determination to seek out in the vast world this mysterious and wonderful substance essential to a meaningful life only to find out, after years of searching, that it is water. Our cultural ethos requires progress that evolves in time and space. With regard to space, our value system is vertical, like

---

12. Robert Johnson, *HE: Understanding Masculine Psychology* (New York: Harper & Row, 1989).

a ladder, with heaven at the top and hell at its bottom. We measure our accomplishments stretching horizontally in space, with powerful core territories and dependent peripheral satellites. With regard to time, our value system reaches back and forth unremittingly, never becoming still in the present moment. Everything is either better or worse than it was or not as good or as bad as it could get. It is no wonder that the cross, one vertical and one horizontal line that intercross, has long been emblematic of Western might. Sharp angles, either or neither, black or white, this binary mode of speculation fueled the astounding late fifteenth-and sixteenth-century voyages of European discovery as well as produced the fantastic technological marvels of applied science of the twentieth and twenty-first centuries we take so much for granted today.

The ethos of modern living has transmitted to us the legacy of the explorer. Travelers of all kinds and affiliations, throughout the history of Western civilization, have envisioned themselves as explorers and conquerors. Even in our current age of mass tourism, one has only to look at tourism brochures or watch and listen to tourism promotion on television to agree that little has changed since the heyday of European exploration. A twenty-first-century tourist still wants to explore virgin territories and to conquer the world. But because there are no more virgin territories to visit (the last unknown lands on earth to be explored were the North Pole, reached by the American Robert Peary in 1909, and the South Pole, reached by the Norwegian Roald Anundsen in 1911), and because the world has already been conquered, unconquered, and reconquered, tourism promoters sell their concepts of paradise on earth and of land conquests neatly packaged and labeled with such names as the "Perfect Evasion" or the "Authentic Experience." However, parallel to the legacy of the explorer, Travelers and we contemporary tourists have also inherited the notion that the purpose of any journey is the process of traveling, or the journey itself. The process is what matters. This mantra has been repeated over and over again by Travelers; it is a distinct although weaker soundtrack but one nonetheless clearly heard in the background of all notable or modest voyages. This tradition favors the symbol of the circle over that of the cross, the circle with a dot in the middle. Our position on the circle matters little since any placement around it is precisely at the same distance from the center; wherever we move on the circle, we are always at the exact same distance from its center. What matters is the movement itself or, more accurately, the knowing that the center remains unchanged by our movement on the circle. Travel on the circle is a journey whenever and wherever time and space vanish into the awareness of the center. A Traveler on a journey becomes the dot in the middle of the circle and the circle itself.

In life as in travel, I like to think of the center of the circle as the epiphany. The epiphany is the point at which we are transformed. From the center of the circle we have equal access to any conceivable position on the circle. What, then, do we find at the center? Who or what is at the center of the universe? Could it be that we find at the center the *anima mundi*, the living soul of the universe? Could it be that the living soul of the universe is who we are, each and every one of us? Could it be where we awake from the dream we share? Is there such a thing as a prototypical journey? Are the essential features of the journey, in which all imaginable journeys throughout man's history may be rooted, to be found in the secret nature of the center of the circle? Do we Travelers follow commanding directives, perhaps molecular imperatives, exhorting us to initiate the journey? Are we human beings on a journey that takes us beyond any journey, beyond all journeys? We like to say that life is a journey. But what if the journey is life? And what if life is eternal? What is eternity?

Most of us believe that there are economic and historical forces shaping the world. Marx (1818–1883) brilliantly exposed the nature of these forces. Most of us also believe in Darwin's (1809–1882) theory of natural selection and the survival of the fittest or in Freud's (1856–1939) impulsive forces of the subconscious. Those are hypothetical frameworks we accept as part of our everyday reality. What about the imperative of the personal journey? What of the molecular memory compelling us to journey? This is another hypothesis, certainly, but one that may expand our reality. How would we conduct our lives if we unreservedly knew that what matters is the journey and the awareness we bring to it?

Advice to Would-Be Travelers

Remember, you are the journey.

Epilogue: The Life Well Lived

I was at home on State Street Drive in New Orleans. It was mid-August 2006, the height of the hurricane season. I never used to pay attention to this unsavory season. I didn't even know it was a season. In Québec we have four distinct seasons. In post-Katrina New Orleans, we have two: the hurricane season and the other season.

Katrina and Rita had disrupted my family's quiet life in the Big Easy as they did for hundreds of thousands of other people in the city and the Gulf Coast region. I felt disoriented. I was sad. Katrina had washed away the comfortable worn-out sandal fit I used to experience living here. The flow had run dry. I was barefoot scrubbing my house, my street, my neighborhood, and my city.

But I was still a Traveler. That is why I tried to make sense of my life at this particular time and in this particular place through my travel experiences around the world. The rapidity of travel today, its ease and apparent benign character, belies its formidable nature as an agent of personal transformation. Travelers actively seek personal transformations. On occasion, though, we get more than we bargained for.

Sometimes without noticing it, but at other times with full awareness of the process we are engaged in, we are confronted with the task of integration, of making sense of all our travel experiences. At times the pace of change is too fast, and indigestion follows. I remember one evening I checked into a cheap hotel on Kowloon peninsula in Hong Kong after traveling for many months and had a very disquieting experience. I woke up in my small, windowless, stinking room in the middle of the night, and for a moment I had absolutely no idea where I was. What place was this? What city was it? What country?

Unable to find the answers to these simple questions, I panicked for a brief moment and rushed out of the room, looking for a clue to calm me down. I couldn't recognize anything, and the bare walls were of no help. I made my way to the desk, looked at the Philippine girl half-asleep on her chair, and feeling too awkward to ask a direct question, I asked if she had a hotel card. I needed the phone number, I said. She handed one to me. It was only when I looked at it that I knew I was in Hong Kong. I went back to bed thinking that I needed to slow down the pace of my travels; that I needed time to integrate my recent fast-paced traveling experiences.

I felt the same way about my life in New Orleans in 2006. I would wake up in the morning and often wondered what had happened to the last months or the last year. It was a blur, a heartrending blur. I was dizzy. Living in New Orleans then felt exactly like waking up in that room in the middle of the night in Hong Kong.

Hurricanes are spectacular agents of personal transformation that literally take us beyond our rational minds. The entire experience leaves us drained and confused. And it is hard to bring such an experience to a close. Perhaps it is impossible to do so. It stays with us forever. Just like the tsunami in Southeast Asia. What happened and is still happening to the countless lives touched by the disruptive force of the tsunami? It could have affected my life, as I've been to many of the places destroyed by the tsunami. Katrina did affect my life.

Back to travel. In a few places, such as the beautiful beach of Zipolite in the state of Oaxaca in Mexico, the world of Travelers is sometimes turned upside down. Zipolite attracts all kinds of Travelers, but mostly the hippie type of Traveler, the ones with very little money but with a desire to live there for a long time on almost nothing. An exceptionally beautiful setting, a thriving drug scene, nudity, dangerous squabbles (sometimes deadly) and very cheap accommodations ensure that Zipolite remains a unique travel destination that attracts mostly Travelers, especially the Travelers who desire to let go of everything.

Thefts are regularly reported in Zipolite, many of them committed by Travelers. Death by drowning is not uncommon. The first time I went to Zipolite, a Norwegian man drowned in the afternoon, and a German woman reported a rape that same day. Mexican anthropologist Juan Carlo told me that many longtime temporary residents of Zipolite are foreigners or Mexicans fleeing legal problems in their respective cities or countries. Things sometimes get rough there, and even regular visitors to Zipolite, such as a Québec couple I met in San Patricio-Melaque, say they sometimes avoid going there when things get out of hand.

"We decided not to stay," said Pierre. "We love the place, but this time it was out of control. Half the foreigners get robbed!"

Nevertheless, to be fair to Zipolite, almost all Travelers I talked to who have been there reported no problems at all. All were enthralled by the magic of the place, and most had enjoyed feeling the sun on their entire body or trying the ever-popular hallucinogenic mushrooms (you can get a magic mushroom omelet at many local restaurants). Zipolite is always high on the Traveler's must-see list in Mexico: "Fabled as southern Mexico's ultimate place to lie back in a hammock and do as little as you like, for almost as little as you like." (*Lonely Planet: Mexico*, 1995). Drugs and nudity are the main magnets.

Perhaps New Orleans of 2006 was going through a similar experience when the world seems to be turned upside down even though it was still the same. Or was it? "Will New Orleans be the same?" I was often asked this question. My answer: "If you were diagnosed with terminal cancer today and survived the ordeal, would you be the same person?" I hope not. Why go through such difficult times if you are not transforming yourself in the process and becoming a healthier, more compassionate human being? This particular experience ought to be a facet of the life well lived. I am determined to live my life well. We live in a dangerous world. But the dangerous world is a very safe place if we only acknowledge the true nature of danger: its transformative power. People often say to me that it must have been a very dangerous endeavor to travel the world as I did, by myself, for such a long period of time. But it wasn't. Ask any Traveler. However, I did find myself in tight situations a few times when my life could have been in danger. Most Travelers have similar stories. It comes with the territory. But, overall, traveling around the world is very safe when one feels at home in the world.

It is easier now in 2012 to feel at home in New Orleans. This warm, deeply felt feeling has come back.

However, to this day, strong and unsettling emotions run through all of us who live in the city. Even though we know, deep inside, that emotions are not who we are, that we are infinitely more than what we feel and experience at any particular time in our lives, we also have to understand that emotions do fashion who we become. In other words, we do have to recognize, express, and process the compelling conflicting emotions we all felt and still feel just by breathing the air in New Orleans.

Experiences such as Katrina or the 2004 Christmas tsunami are never over for the people whose lives have been changed by them. They continue to transform lives. Travel also continues to transform lives. My story as a Traveler is ongoing. Deep inside I am still the same Traveler who boarded a plane to Vancouver thirty-five years ago. That is the beauty of it: to feel the same excitement I did at the Montréal airport when I was eighteen years old. I am exactly the same, only a little older.

Final Advice to Would-Be Travelers

What are you waiting for?

About the Author

Régent Jean Cabana is a passionate Traveler. At age thirty-three his childhood dream of circling the globe became a reality when he began an eighteen-month sojourn traveling solo around the world. Upon his return, he conducted a prolific ethnographic research on Travelers for his Ph.D. dissertation. Cabana teaches comparative urban sociology classes in Mexico, Brazil, and Canada to American and Canadian students. He is also a consultant in academic international programs.

www.ingramcontent.com/pod-product-compliance
Lightning Source LLC
Chambersburg PA
CBHW022022090426

42739CB00006BA/252